THE GRIZZLY ALMANAC

Also by Robert H. Busch

The Wolf Almanac

Wolf Songs: The Classic Collection
of Writing about Wolves (ed.)

The Cougar Almanac

Gray Whales: Wandering Giants

Valley of the Grizzlies

Loons

Salmon Country

THE
GRIZZLY
ALMANAC

Robert H. Busch

THE LYONS PRESS

Designed by Compset, Inc.

Printed in the United States of America

10 9 8 7 6 5 4 3 2 1

Library of Congress Cataloging-in-Publication Data

Busch, Robert.
    The grizzly almanac/Robert H. Busch.
      p. cm.
    Includes bibliographical references (p.).
    ISBN 1-58574-143-4
    1. Grizzly bear. I. Title.
QL737.C27 B858 2000
599.784—dc21

                                              00-058587

For Snoop and Maggie, who share my life.

CONTENTS

PREFACE

To some, the grizzly bear is the ultimate symbol of wilderness. To others, it is the ultimate horror that hides behind every tree.

I saw my first wild grizzly on a hike many years ago to some remote lakes in the backcountry behind Mount Eisenhower in the Canadian Rockies. A winding trail meandered along the rocky edge of the mountain, and it was around one bend in the trail that I suddenly came nose to snout with a grizzly.

Not 30 feet away, the bear stood its ground and stared at me. I stared back, more from shock than from any clever plan. Indeed, the only thought running through my head was *Oh my God, that's a grizzly.*

After a few dreadful moments, the big bear turned its head and regally walked off into the timber. Retreat with dignity. I just stood there, frozen in awe from the experience.

For the rest of my hike, I looked over my shoulder every few minutes, half-expecting to see 500 pounds of fur and muscle charging toward me. Every twig snap became a grizzly hiding in the brush. Every rustle in the leaves was the big beast circling around behind me. I was a mess.

It is because of reactions like mine that the grizzly was nearly wiped off the face of this continent. Ninety-nine percent of its former range in the lower 48 states is now devoid of grizzlies. The grizzly is absent from nearly a quarter of its Canadian range. Yet still the big bear hangs on.

It does so partly because it is an omnivore, capable of eating a wide variety of foods, and partly because it is an opportunist, capable of living in a wide variety of habitats.

Today, the big bear has an admiring fanship where before there was animosity. Its roadside appearances cause mile-long traffic jams in Yellowstone National Park. Clumps of people can be found gathered around the grizzly exhibits in zoos, gasping collectively at the bears' sheer size and at the length of their claws. Biological studies into the big bear abound. Probably only the wolf has been more intensively studied.

But the wild country that the grizzly calls home is being invaded more and more by human influences that negatively impact its future. Ranches creep further and further into the foothills. Roads to oil fields and mining camps crawl along the valleys. Hydropower lines and pipeline rights of way snake over the ridges. And hunters and hikers increasingly invade what little is left of wild America.

Even such innocuous buildings as weekend cabins in the woods can indirectly harm the big bear, for they often are accompanied by improperly disposed garbage. Compost heaps, bird feeders, and fruit trees also cause problems by attracting bears much closer than many people wish.

Unfortunately, a huge tide of paranoia sweeps over many people at the mere mention of the grizzly's name. Alaska's Koyukon Indians used to call the bear *bik'ints'itldaadla*, meaning "keep out of its way," a fitting title for the feared king of the woods.

More recently, in 1998, Idaho Senator Stan Hawkins, speaking at a news conference in a zoo, stated emphatically that "The only place in Idaho we should find dangerous predators who threaten human lives, property, and wildlife is right here, behind bars."

Balancing this type of hysteria is the wealth of observations on the relatively benign nature of the grizzly. In Alberta recently, biologist Robin Munro and pilot John Bell watched hikers on a trail who were unknowingly being watched by a large grizzly not 100 yards away. "The bear just waited until the hikers passed, then it crossed right behind them," said Munro. Most of the time, the big bear means us no harm.

The Grizzly Almanac is an attempt to gather the known facts about grizzly biology and behavior into a volume that can be used by laymen and academics alike. It is also an attempt to separate myth from fact, for, like most predators, the grizzly suffers from an incredibly bad press, often based on old wives' tales and pumped-up hunting stories.

And if the key to the bear's future is education, it is my hope that this book will be one stepping stone in the road to a more secure future for what many believe is the most impressive animal on the continent.

Robert H. Busch

THE GRIZZLY ALMANAC

CHAPTER

1

The Ancient Bear

Grizzly country is wilderness country, and he cannot live without it.

ANDY RUSSELL, 1967

EVOLUTION

A long time ago, in a childhood far, far away, I wrote an essay on fossil jellyfish. I chose the bizarre topic because of the challenging depth of research it would entail. Jellyfish are amorphous little blobs with no internal skeletons or hard parts, so their fossil record and evolution are both a matter of conjecture. Bears, however, have bones, and this simple anatomical fact has allowed paleontologists to reconstruct the grizzly's evolution in some detail.

The first bearlike creatures evolved from small mammals called miacids that lived in the Paleocene through Eocene epochs. Miacids were small arboreal animals that were well equipped as carnivores, with special canine teeth (to hold and pierce prey) and carnassials (to shear off pieces of meat).

Around 60 million years ago, two branches evolved from the miacids: the cat family (aeluroids or viverravines) and the dog family (arctoids or vulpavines). Bears eventually evolved from the dog family, and indeed the closest relatives that wild bears have today are the wild dogs.

The bear's chapter in history began about 34 million years ago, when a small, dog-sized animal called *Cephalogale* appeared in Asia. This animal was a treetop hunter; it pursued small prey through the early forests.

From *Cephalogale* evolved an animal known as *Ursavis elmensis,* or the "dawn bear," a terrier-sized predator that still conducted much of its hunting in the treetops. However, its carnassials were reduced in size, and its posterior molars had developed chewing and grinding surfaces, allowing it to supplement its diet with plant material.

The dawn bear gradually evolved into other members of the genus *Ursavis;* these bear ancestors in turn evolved into a little-known creature called *Protursus.*

Protursus is known from only a few fossils; its original description was based only on a single fossil tooth found in Spain. *Protursus* was about the size of a large wolf.

Somewhere around 5 million years ago, the first member of the *Ursus* genus appeared, probably in southern Europe. This was *Ursus etruscus,* the Etruscan bear. Fossil evidence suggests that this animal was the direct ancestor of brown bears, with large molar teeth that were useful for chewing up vegetation.

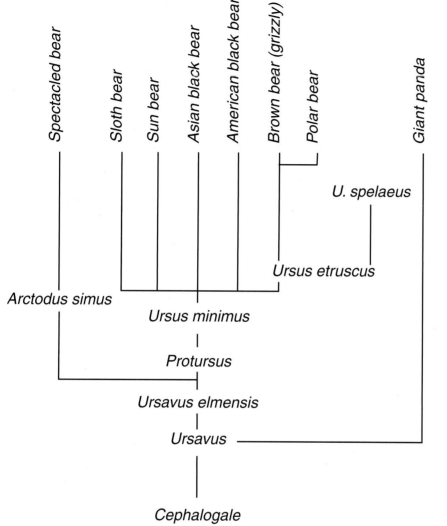

The grizzly family tree.
(after Ward and
Kynaston, 1995)

Most biologists believe that *Ursus etruscus* separated into two distinct lineages—the Asian brown bear and *Ursus speleaus,* the famed and formidable cave bear.

Cave bears were large animals that weighed up to 880 pounds (400 kg). These bears were opportunistic omnivores, eating primarily vegetation. The European brown bear now occupies the same ecological niche. Cave bears were found in the mountainous areas of Germany, France, and Russia. They had a large head, small eyes, and large bones. The cave bear survived through two Ice Ages and did not die out until about 11,000 years ago. The first known relationships

The grizzly is a form of brown bear, a species Holarctic in distribution across North America and Asia. (Robert H. Busch)

between humans and bears are thought to have been between cave bears and Neanderthal humans, in what is now southern Europe.

By around 1.3 million years ago, *Ursus etruscus* had disappeared and *Ursus arctos,* the brown bear, had evolved, perhaps in the area we now know as China. Grizzlies are a form of brown bear.

These early brown bears might never have reached the New World except for a quirk of geology. Today, the northeastern tip of Asia and the northwestern tip of Alaska are separated by 60 miles (90 km) of water that ranges from 100 to 165 feet (30 to 50 m) deep. However, during the most recent Ice Age, as water became locked up in glacial ice caps, the sea level fell by up to 400 feet (125 m), and a strip of land emerged that connected what is now Siberia and Alaska. That tenuous connection, which appeared and disappeared as Ice Ages came and went, provided a crucial route for Asian animals, including early bears, to migrate to North America.

Although early bears had strolled over the Bering land bridge between Asia and North America as early as 1.5 million years ago, evolving into the North American black bear, grizzlies did not follow until much later. How much later is a matter of great debate. The earliest fossil brown bears in North America were found in Alaska; these fossils date to 200,000 years ago, although there may have been earlier bears that left no fossil record.

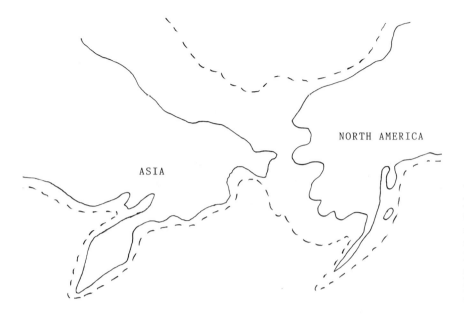

The current edges of North America and Asia (*solid line*) and edges during the last Ice Age (*dashed line*). The lowering of sea level created a connecting land mass called Beringia.

The grizzlies took over the ecological niche formerly occupied by the giant short-faced bear (*Arctodus simus*), which had arrived in North America about 1.3 million years ago. This huge beast was the largest carnivorous land animal ever, standing upright at a height of up to 11 feet (3 m). Its snout was short, leading to its nickname of

The black bear arrived in North America long before the grizzly and is far more numerous today. (Jean Capps/DragonSnaps)

Polar bears are thought to have evolved from an isolated population of brown bears somewhere along the Siberian coast. (Robert H. Busch)

bulldog bear. It had a low forehead, long legs, and weighed almost a ton, making the bulldog bear a powerful predator.

There in fact were a number of large, bearlike animals living on both the North American and Asian continents prior to the Ice Age. This is an example of what is called *convergent evolution,* the trend for similar-appearing animals to evolve in different areas.

The giant short-faced bear and its cousins finally became extinct in the mid-Pleistocene Period. The most likely reason for their demise is increasing competition from the brown bears, which spread rapidly across the continent.

Many biologists believe that about 10,000 to 100,000 years ago, some of the brown bears in the far north became isolated, and gradually lost their brown coats and developed whiter coats that helped them blend in better with their Arctic habitat. Eventually they evolved into the polar bear (*Ursus maritimus*). This evolution is thought to have taken place somewhere along the northern Siberian coast.

The polar bear is unique in that it has almost no Ice Age fossil record. The sole polar bear fossils of that era are a few bits of bone about 20,000 years old. The polar bear is also unusual in that it is the only bear that is almost completely carnivorous, depending primarily on seals for its food. The polar bear is also the only bear with a semi-aquatic lifestyle.

A few zoos have reported successful matings between polar and grizzly bears, proof of their close relationship. The offspring of these matches are often fertile, another clue that the polar bear and grizzly bear are "kissing cousins."

It has been theorized that much of the grizzly's reknowned surly attitude may have arisen as a result of its evolution in the treeless tundra of the far north. Black bears, the theory goes, evolved further south, where they always had trees to which to escape. Grizzlies weren't so lucky, and therefore had to evolve a more aggressive behavior in order to survive.

TAXONOMY

Grizzlies belong to Kingdom Animalia, Phylum Chordata, Class Mammalia, Order Carnivora, Family Ursidae, and the genus *Ursus.* Grizzly speciation and subspeciation, however, are two of the fuzziest of bear topics.

The grizzly was first classed as *Ursus arctos* in 1758 by Carolus Linnaeus (Carl von Linné), the Swedish naturalist who developed a binomial nominclature for species that is still in use today.

In 1815, Philadelphia naturalist George Ord dubbed the grizzly *Ursus horribilis,* Latin for "horrible bear." He based his description on information provided by the Lewis and Clark expedition, which crossed the waist of the continent in 1804 and 1805 and managed to kill over 40 grizzlies in the process. The type locality for the species was the Missouri River in Montana. No type specimen was designated.

Naturalist Adelbert von Chamisso theorized in 1815 that the grizzly was the same species as the European brown bear, but it was not until 1851 that Russian biologist Alexander Theodor von Middendorff recognized that the brown bear was a Holarctic species ranging across much of the Northern Hemisphere. Middendorff renamed the bear *Ursus arctos horribilis,* which is Latin for "horrible northern bear."

When biologist C. Hart Merriam, director of the United States Bureau of Biological Survey, published his epic *Review of Grizzly and Big Brown Bears of North America* in 1918, he listed no fewer than 86 separate species and subspecies, using tiny differences in skull measurements as the basis for his classification. In some cases, he used a single skull as the basis for naming a new species, flimsy evidence in-

There are two subspecies of grizzly: *Ursus arctos horribilis,* like this Canadian grizzly, and *Ursus arctos middendorfi,* the giant Kodiak bear of Alaska. (Robert H. Busch)

deed for such an undertaking. There was a Canada grizzly, an Apache grizzly, a flat-headed grizzly, a strange grizzly, a thick-set grizzly and even an industrious grizzly. In Alaska alone, Merriam described over 20 subspecies.

Today, only one species and two subspecies are recognized. Biologist R. L. Rausch in 1953 divided all grizzlies into two subspecies—*Ursus arctos middendorffi* and *Ursus arctos horribilis. Ursus arctos middendorffi,* Latin for "northern Middendorff bear," is the big Alaskan brown bear or Kodiak bear. Rausch stated his contention that Kodiaks are found only on the Kodiak, Afognak, and Shuyak islands along the southern coast of Alaska. This subspecies likely evolved about 10,000 years ago when glaciation cut off the island chain from the mainland. Kodiaks have a wide face and high skull. They number about 3,000 bears today. Kodiaks are the largest of grizzlies, growing to enormous sizes on rich diets of salmon and berries.

The other subspecies Rausch designated is *Ursus arctos horribilis,* a catch-all that includes all the other grizzlies in North America, including the large coastal grizzlies of the Alaskan Peninsula.

Scientists are not the only ones interested in the big bears. For many years, hunters recognized a difference between the huge

Alaskan Kodiak bear and other grizzlies, but physical distinctions were hazy and subspecies boundaries quite arbitrary.

America's largest hunting club, the Boone and Crockett Club, for example, drew a line 75 miles (114 km) from the Alaskan coast and declared that coastal bears within this line were browns and those on the other side were grizzlies.

To replace that imaginary line, the Club now uses a precise geographic description, stating that north and east of this line, bear trophies are regarded as grizzlies, not Kodiaks. The boundary line is defined as "Starting at Pearse Canal and following the Canadian-Alaskan boundary to Mt. Natazhat; thence west northwest along the divide of the Wrangell Range to Mt. Jarvis at the western edge of the Wrangell Range; thence north along along the divide of the Mentasta Range to Mentasta Pass; thence in a general westerly direction along the divide of the Alaskan Range to Houston Pass; thence westerly following the 62nd parallel of latitude to the Bering Sea" (Byers and Bettas, 1999).

The Boone and Crockett Club now says that Kodiaks "are found on Kodiak and Afognak Island, the Alaskan Peninsula, and eastward and southeastward along the coast of Alaska. The smaller interior grizzly is found in the remaining parts of the continent" (Byers and Bettas, 1999). So to many hunters, the grizzlies of coastal mainland Alaska are Kodiaks; to biologists, they are grizzlies.

Perhaps the most colorful taxonomic description of all came from biologist Theodore Walker, who once said that "the grizzly, of course, is nothing more than an underfed Alaskan brown."

THE MYSTERY OF THE UNGAVA BEAR

Despite biologists who scoff at such a notion, there is a substantial body of evidence suggesting that a subspecies of grizzly once inhabited the remote forests of northern Quebec and eastern Labrador.

In 1550, French cartographer Pierre Desceliers drew the Desceliers Map, which shows three bears along the coast of Labrador. One is white and is obviously a polar bear, but the other two are brown. Both are the same size as the polar bear. According to the experts, only black bears and polar bears inhabit the region.

In the late 1700s, Captain George Cartwright, one of the first English settlers in Labrador, wrote of a bear species in the area

Young grizzlies often have a collar of white fur, which they lose as they age. (Jean Capps/DragonSnaps)

that was quite different from the polar and black bears, describing it as "a kind of bear very ferocious, having a white ring around its neck." Young grizzlies (see photo) often have such a marking.

Modern natives of the area tell of the Great Bear of the Montagnais, a large, brown, and dangerous bear that used to live as far south as the Mealy Mountains of southern Labrador.

By the 19th century, the Hudson Bay Company had trading posts along the coast of Labrador and northern Quebec. One of its traders, John Maclean, worked for the Bay for six years at Fort Chimo on the southern shore of Ungava Bay. In his district report for 1837 to 1838, he lists three types of bear skins: black, Arctic (polar), and "grissle." And this description was from a trader who had spent four years in British Columbia and knew well what a "grissle" bear's hide looked like. He noted in a book about his years at Ungava Bay that "when we consider the great extent of country that intervenes between Ungava and the far west, it seems inexplicable that the grisly bear should be found in so insulated a situation . . . the fact of their being there, however, does not admit of a doubt, for I have traded and sent to England several of their skins."

But is it really so unusual to expect a grizzly 500 miles (758 km) east of its regular range? In the far north, grizzlies have been found 300 miles (455 km) north of where biologists say they should be, and there is really no reason that grizzlies could not have spread from Southampton Island—their known easternmost limit—east to the coast of northen Quebec at one time.

And the trading records are hard to dispute. For example, Hudson Bay records for 1839 at Fort Chimo record that 1 black bear skin and 4 "grey bears" skins were traded. The Hudson Bay Company was the acknowledged expert in furtrading in Canada, so it is unlikely that one of its traders would be confused when it came to bear skins.

Captain William Kennedy, who worked in the Ungava District in the 1860s, stated that a variety of grizzly skins were traded at the Fort Chimo, Fort Nascapie, and George River posts.

In addition to the Hudson Bay posts, there were a string of Moravian missions along the Labrador coast. Their records show that the Moravians had regularly traded skins of "grey" or "grizzly" bears for many decades, buying the last one in 1914. Indeed, by the late 1800s it appeared that the Ungava brown bear was becoming rare.

Ethnologist L. M. Turner stayed at Fort Chimo from 1882 to 1884 and stated that "the brown or barren-ground bear appears to be restricted to a narrow area and is not plentiful."

A. P. Lowe, a geologist who visited Labrador between 1892 and 1895, reported that "specimens of the barren-ground bear are obtained only at infrequent intervals . . . skins are brought at intervals to Fort Chimo where the Indians have a favorable chance to kill [one of these bears]. On other occasions they leave it alone, having a great respect for, and fear, of its ferocity and size."

Around 1900, an independent trader named Martin Hunter, who owned a trading post on Anticosti Island in the Gulf of St. Lawrence, bought some large brown bear skins that came from southern Labrador. He reported that they were of "immense size . . . One skin I got measured seven feet [2 m] broad by nine feet [3 m] long."

In the winter of 1905, American traveler Dillon Wallace spent some time at Fort Chimo and reported that "a very large and ferocious brown bear . . . inhabits the barrens to the eastward of

George River." He stated that traders told him "the hair was very long, light brown in color, silver tipped and of a very different species from either the polar or black bear."

The Ungava brown bear, whatever species or subspecies it was, appears to have died out by the early 1900s. Intriguing evidence of its former existence came to light in 1975, however, when Harvard anthropologist Steven Cox unearthed the skull of a young female bear while excavating a late 18th-century Inuit midden at Okak Bay on the Labrador coast. The skull was identified as that of a grizzly.

RANGE AND HABITAT

The word "grizzly" is only applied to those members of the brown bear family that live in North America. The brown bear has a world-wide distribution, which includes Europe, the Russian Federation, and North America, the largest distribution of any bear species. The Russian Federation is estimated to have the highest brown bear population of all, with over 100,000 bears. Appropriately, the brown bear is the symbol of Russia.

In a 1990 volume entitled *The Status and Conservation of the Bears of the World,* U.S. Fish and Wildlife Service grizzly biologist Chris Servheen wrote that the future of the brown bear "can only be assured in the northeastern and northwestern Soviet Union, Alaska and Canada," a depressing opinion for those enthralled with the great bear.

In North America, the grizzly was once present across a wide swath of the continent (see map) from Alaska to central Mexico, where it was known as *el oso plateado,* "the silvery bear." According to the fossil record as well as reports from reliable observers, it was never present on Vancouver Island, on the Queen Charlotte Islands off the British Columbia coast, nor on most of the Baja peninsula.

The grizzly's range today is a mere remnant of its past distribution. Ninety-nine percent of the grizzlies in the lower 48 states are now gone; almost one-quarter of their Canadian range is now lost. The grizzly today is absent from most of the western United States, Manitoba and Saskatchewan in Canada, the Aleutian Islands west of Unimak Island, the Yukon-Kuskokwin delta region of western Alaska, the northernmost coast of Alaska, and probably all of Mexico.

Historic limit (*dashed line*) and current distribution (*stippled*) of the grizzly bear.

The main ecocenters of population for the grizzly today in the lower 48 states are the Greater Yellowstone Ecosystem and the Northern Continental Divide Ecosystem. The former area is centered around Yellowstone National Park and includes about 18 million acres of national parks, national forests, national wildife refuges, and private land. It is home to between 400 and 600 grizzlies.

The 5.7-million-acre Northern Continental Divide Ecosystem is centered on Glacier National Park. This area is home range for 300 to 600 grizzlies. About 15 percent of the land in the Northern Continental Divide Ecosystem is private land, compared to about 1.5 percent in the Greater Yellowstone Ecosystem.

Three other pockets of grizzly habitat exist today in the lower 48 states. The Selkirk Mountains of Idaho and Washington support perhaps 40 to 50 elusive grizzlies, and perhaps 30 to 40 more still lurk in the Cabinet-Yaak area of northern Idaho. The North Cascade Mountains of western Washington may support a half-dozen grizzlies at most.

The Northern Continental Divide, Selkirk, and Cabinet-Yaak populations are all contiguous with grizzly populations in Alberta and British Columbia. In the early 1990s, the B.C. Wildlife Branch augmented the Cabinet-Yaak grizzly population by supplying four subadult female grizzlies from British Columbia, one of which is known to have since died.

Recently, researchers have discovered a migration of bears between the Selkirk and Cabinet-Yaak ecosystems. Many biologists are now recommending that the two should be considered as a single grizzly bear zone.

One of these areas may in fact now be devoid of the great bear; the last confirmed grizzly kill in the North Cascades took place in 1967, and although the area is contiguous with known grizzly habitat in Canada, the presence of a self-perpetuating population of grizzlies in Washington state has yet to be confirmed. Intensive searching in the early 1990s found only one set of grizzly tracks in the area.

By political jurisdiction, in the lower 48 states, Montana has about 800 grizzlies, Wyoming about 250, Idaho about 30, and Washington around a half-dozen.

Alaska today harbors about 32,000 grizzlies. As huge as this number sounds, it is best to remember Aldo Leopold's famous comment

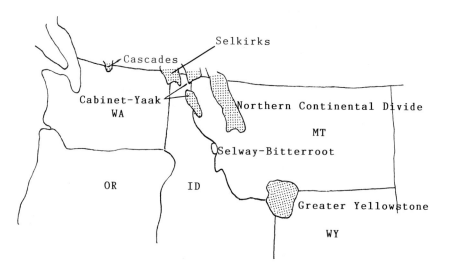

Grizzly ecosystems (*shaded*) and potential reintroduction sites (*unshaded*) in the northwest United States.

from his classic, *A Sand County Almanac:* "Relegating grizzlies to Alaska is about like relegating happiness to heaven; one may never get there."

One of the last strongholds for the American grizzly was the mountainous state of Colorado. In 1952, government trapper Lloyd Anderson killed a female grizzly whose two cubs escaped. Many thought she was the last grizzly in Colorado. Officials set up the Rio Grande-San Juan Grizzly Bear Management Area in 1954, in hopes of preserving this last island of grizzly habitat. But ten years later, the management area was dissolved, after "experts" decreed that no positive evidence of grizzly bear inhabitation had been found.

However, on September 23, 1979, conservationists were amazed when big game outfitter Ed Wiseman, of Crestone, Colorado, killed a 16-year-old female grizzly in the San Juan Mountains. Wiseman stated that he had been guiding bowhunting client Mike Nierderee of Kansas when he was charged by the bear. Wiseman then stabbed the bear in the throat with an arrow, killing her on the spot. However, there was also an arrow wound in the bear's shoulder, leading many to suspect that the bear had been wounded first.

A field examination of the bear revealed enlarged mammaries, suggesting that she may have had a litter in the recent past. The bear was estimated at no more than 20 years old, making her too young to have been one of the escaped cubs from Lloyd Anderson's 1952 kill. Her skull and hide were recovered, but two efforts at lifting out her carcass resulted in two crashed helicopters. As author Rick Bass pointed out in an *Audubon* magazine article on Colorado's grizzlies, "The mountain would not entirely give up what was hers, and what had always been hers" (Bass, 1993).

In 1996, four grizzlies were found in the Wind River range near the Green River headwaters in Wyoming, the southernmost grizzly sighting since the 1979 killing in Colorado. The four bears were quickly relocated for their own sake to a safer area closer to Yellowstone National Park.

It is unlikely that the small clumps of grizzly habitat in Idaho, Washington, and perhaps Colorado will last much longer. Biologist Mark Shaffer, who wrote his doctoral thesis at Duke University on the Yellowstone grizzly, wrote about the patches of remaining grizzly habitat in *Keeping the Grizzly Bear in the American West*, a pamphlet published, appropriately enough, by the Wilderness Society. He described the pockets of habitats as "an archipelago of isolated population remnants, none of which is sufficiently large to be viable in its own right."

Shaffer found that under normal circumstances, once a grizzly population drops below 50 to 90 bears, that population is inevitably headed for extinction. None of the bear populations in Idaho, Washington, or Colorado is even close to that number.

Mexico's last grizzlies took to the rugged mountains of that country in the 1950s. The last grizzly killed in the Sierra Madre range was killed in 1932. A vigorous poisoning campaign in the late 1950s and early 1960s may have killed off any stragglers in the more remote corners of the country. Mexico's last documented grizzly was apparently killed in 1960, in the Sierra del Nido range in the state of Chihuahua, although undocumented kills were reported in 1964, 1965, and 1967. A thorough search of the area in 1968 and again in 1979 was unable to find any grizzly sign. The International Union for the Conservation of Nature and Natural Resources (IUCN) considers the Mexican grizzly to be extinct.

The record in Canada has not been as bleak for grizzlies and their habitat. As Thomas McNamee wrote in *The Grizzly Bear,* "Canadians seem never to have harried their varmints with quite the same addled glee as the Americans." In Canada, grizzlies still occupy three-quarters of their original range, with over 20,000 grizzlies surviving today. The Northwest Territories has about 4,800 grizzlies, the Yukon about 6,000 to 7,000, British Columbia 10,000 to 13,000 and Alberta around 800.

In Canada's north, grizzlies range right up to the northern edge of the continent, with a few sightings of lone animals on the Arctic islands. Grizzlies were reported by Inuit hunters on Southampton Island at the northern end of Hudson Bay, in both 1948 and 1950. As recently as the 1960s, biologists reported significant numbers of grizzlies in the Thelon River area of the central Northwest Territories.

In the far north, there are six documented sightings on the southern part of Victoria Island. One grizzly was shot on Banks Island in the winter of 1951 to 1952, and there are reports of two more recent sightings. In 1991, a big male grizzly was spotted in Viscount Melville Sound, some 300 miles (455 km) north of its usual range. Most of these sightings were of lone males that evidently wandered far north in pursuit of seals.

Although the grizzly is primarily considered an animal of the forest, the bear can inhabit a wide variety of habitats, including dry grassland such as this area in British Columbia. (Robert H. Busch)

Most of the blame for the decline of the grizzly can be attributed to habitat loss. Grizzlies are extremely adaptable animals, capable of inhabiting a wide variety of habitats, from barren plains to frigid alpine valleys. The key element is food availability, which has resulted in such rich areas as riparian zones, floodplains, and avalanche chutes being areas also rich in grizzlies.

Avalanche chutes—narrow areas that have been stripped by rock or snowslides—are especially popular. In a study of 19 radio-collared grizzlies in the Swan Mountains of northwestern Montana, biologists John Waller and Richard Mace found that avalanche chutes were used in a higher proportion than other available habitat types in the area. The popularity of the chutes may be due to the presence of favored vegetation in riparian areas within the chutes, or to the availability of animal carcasses in the avalanche areas.

Habitat usage is often seasonal, with many bears emerging from winter hibernation to travel down to lowlands to feed upon new spring vegetation, then moving to higher elevations in summer to feed in avalanche chutes and remote alpine areas. The bears then often wander down to lowlands again in the late summer and fall, to gorge on berries and salmon.

The home ranges of most grizzlies thus include a patchwork of several dissimilar habitat types. Mixed shrubland and conifer forests

Rich valley bottoms are prime grizzly habitat. (Robert H. Busch)

are particularly well used because they provide both sufficient food and adequate cover. In one study in Yellowstone National Park, radio-collared grizzlies were located in wooded habitats 90 percent of the time (Blanchard, 1983). So, if you're looking for bears, look in the woods.

CHAPTER

2

The Big Bear

*. . . a verry large and a turrible
looking animal.*

LEWIS AND CLARK, 1805

SIZE AND WEIGHT

Much of the awe inspired by the grizzly is due to its sheer size. Naturalist John Muir accurately described the grizzly as "the sequoia of the animals" in his 1901 book, *Our National Parks*.

The heaviest documented grizzly appears to be one shot on Kodiak Island in 1894, which weighed 1,656 pounds (753 kg). Grizzlies over 1,000 pounds (2,200 kg) are very rare; campfire tales of 2,000-plus-pound trophies are pure fantasy. As Adolph Murie once pointedly wrote, "A bear a long distance from a scale always weighs the most" (Murie, 1961).

This was recognized as early as 1860 by pioneer mountaineer "Grizzly" Adams, who was quoted in the book *The Adventures of James C. Adams, Mountaineer and Grizzly Bear Hunter of California* as stating that "the grizzly of the Rocky Mountains seldom, if ever, reaches a weight of a thousand pounds."

The largest Yellowstone National Park grizzly was an 1,120-pound (509-kg) fatso that gained his pear-shaped figure after a steady diet of human garbage at dumps. Most Yellowstone males are 215 to 715 pounds (98 to 325 kg); females are 200 to 450 pounds (91 to 205 kg). In a tabulation of grizzly bear weights across North America in 1987

With abundant food, grizzlies can grow to over a thousand pounds. (Karl Sommerer)

(Interagency Grizzly Bear Committee) the average male weighed 442 pounds (205 kg) and the average female weighed 290 pounds (132 kg). A similar tabulation from the southwest Yukon in Canada revealed an average weight of 306 pounds (139 kg) for mature males and 209 pounds (95 kg) for mature females (Pearson, 1975).

Male grizzlies are impressive beasts that can stretch 8 feet (2 m) from nose to tail, with a heart girth of 82 inches (208 cm). The average Yellowstone grizzly stands 3½ to 4½ feet (1.0 to 1.4 m) high at the shoulders, with a nose-to-tail length of 77½ inches (197 cm) for males and 70 inches (178 cm) for females.

One way to distinguish between the sexes, aside from size, is by watching grizzlies urinate. The female grizzly's stream of urine jets backward from the hind end, whereas the male's jets forward, toward the front paws.

Despite their great weight, grizzlies are surprisingly light on their feet. In terms of pounds supported per square inch of foot area, a grizzly's foot supports less than one-fifth the weight supported by a deer's foot. This gives the bear an obvious advantage in chasing prey over snow.

Along with a great size comes an awesome strength. A big male grizzly may have claws almost 4 inches (10 cm) long (see photos) and canine teeth 2 inches (5 cm) in length, all of which are used as mighty meathooks.

The front claws of an adult grizzly can reach four inches in length. (Robert H. Busch)

A close-up look at the claws of a young grizzly. (Jean Capps/ DragonSnaps)

Alberta bear biologist Gordon Stenhouse once watched a large grizzly running effortlessly down a steep mountain slope carrying a 300-pound (136-kg) sheep in its mouth. "The power of these animals is just awesome," he says (quoted in Struzik, 1999).

One might think that such a bulky beast would be easy to out-run. In fact, over a short distance, an angry grizzly can easily reach 35 miles (53 km) per hour. One sow grizzly in the Cascade Valley north of Banff, Alberta, chased a truck full of park wardens at a maximum speed of just over 40 miles (61 km) per hour for a short distance before she returned to her two cubs. Another grizzly, in Denali National Park, Alaska, was clocked at 41 miles (62 km) per hour.

Many people believe that grizzlies, because of their great size, cannot climb trees. As many unfortunate people have discovered, this is not true. It is true that a grizzly's front claws are only slightly curved compared to those of a black bear. As a result, grizzlies are not as adept at tree-climbing as their smaller cousins. One of the first to note this was explorer-botanist David Douglas (for whom the Douglas fir is named), who flatly declared in 1824, "this species of bear cannot climb trees."

This belief was echoed by Prince Maximilian of Wied, who traveled up the Missouri on a hunting trip in 1833 and wrote, "This

COLOR

Although most grizzlies are a medium brown color, almost every shade from sandy blonde through mahogany has been recorded. Some bears sport a snazzy, two-tone coat with darker paws and ears, like that of some giant Siamese cat.

One Montana study by Greer and Craighead (1971) found that 50 percent of the grizzlies there were grizzled, 30 percent were dark brown, and 20 percent were light brown. A similar study in the southwest Yukon (Pearson, 1975) found that 72 percent of the grizzlies there were brown to dark brown and 28 percent were light brown or blonde.

Although black bears (*Ursus americanus*) can also be brown, the two bears can be distinguished by the grizzly's greater size, the presence of the grizzly's shoulder hump of muscle, and the grizzly's typically dish-shaped face. The black bear tends to have a shorter, more rounded muzzle. The two bears can also be distinguished by attitude: As an old hunting story goes, if the bear climbs up a tree after you, it's a black bear; if it rips the tree out of the ground, it's a grizzly!

The typical grizzled appearance that led to the grizzly's name is the result of the silver-tipped guard hairs scattered throughout the bear's coat. (The word grizzly actually comes from the Old French term *grisel,* meaning "grayish.") These guard hairs may be up to 4

The Roman nose of an adult grizzly. (Robert H. Busch)

27

The dish-shaped profile of a grizzly's head is obvious in this photo. (Robert H. Busch)

inches (10 cm) long and serve to shed rain and add insulation to the bear's coat.

There do not appear to be any documented records of an albino grizzly, although the Kermode bear, a white subspecies of black bear

Most grizzlies in British Columbia are a dark brown color. (Robert H. Busch)

A rare photo showing the short tail of the grizzly. (Jean Capps/DragonSnaps)

found off British Columbia's coast, is often mistakenly called a "white grizzly."

Grizzlies shed their fur annually, usually between June and August. "At this time of molt," wrote naturalist Andy Russell in *Grizzly Country,* "grizzlies take on the look of mountain hoboes—ragged, unkempt, and tattered." Discarded fur is often used by squirrels in den-linings.

Bringing up the rear of the grizzly's body is a stubby 2- to 7-inch (5-cm to 18-cm)-long tail. Few people, however, get close enough to the bears to see it.

TEETH

Grizzlies have 42 teeth, with three incisors, one canine, four premolars, and two molar teeth on each side of the upper jaw. On each side of the lower jaw are three incisors, one canine, four premolars, and three molars. Some or all of the first three upper and lower premolars often fall out as the bear ages.

The canines are used to pierce and hold prey and may reach 1½ inches (4 cm) in length. The incisors are used to bite off bits of food, and the molars to crush vegetation.

A close look at the molars provides a good clue to grizzly's diet. In most carnivores, the molars are *carnassial,* which means they are

The long canine teeth of the grizzly are often visible from a distance and may exceed 2 inches (5 cm) in length. (Robert H. Busch)

sharply pointed, designed to shear off bits of meat. But in grizzlies, the molars are *occludal,* meaning they are broad with flat crowns, an adaptation for crushing vegetation.

Whereas on human molars there is a regular pattern of bumps and hollows, on a grizzly's molars the surface is irregular, as if carnassials had been modified, which is what has happened during the evolution of the bear.

By the age of 8 months, a grizzly cub has its first and second pairs of incisors, all its premolars, and the upper and lower molars. By 15 months, the third pair of incisors are in place and the upper and lower second molars are erupting.

Grizzlies can be aged by counting the tooth rings, very similar to tree rings in appearance. This was known as early as 1860 by John "Grizzly" Adams, who wrote, "every year a ring is added to its tusks," an amazing observation for an unschooled outdoorsman. Biologists studying grizzlies often remove a tooth from an anesthetized bear, a technique that was first used for mammals in 1950 and for grizzlies in 1964. Rings very close together in the teeth of a female bear often indicate a period of lactation. Dark layers usually indicate a period of winter dormancy. Clear layers are deposited during the summer months.

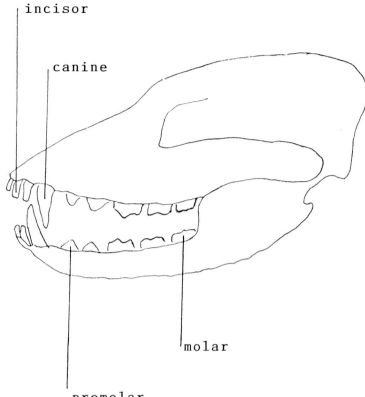

incisor

canine

premolar

molar

Grizzly dentition.

Note the broken canine in the mouth of the bear in front, a common sight in older bears. This bear is in his twenties. (Robert H. Busch)

It is usually a premolar, whose removal does not harm the bear, that is used for sectioning. The age is determined by adding one to the number of annuli (rings) in the tooth cementum.

The length of the teeth, especially the canines, is also a rough guide to age, as canines wear rapidly relative to other teeth and may even break off, especially in older bears.

SCAT

Grizzly scat is usually thick with blunt ends, ranging from 1¼ to 2¾ inches (3.2 to 7.0 cm) in diameter. It is usually broken into segments from 1 to 5 inches (2.5 to 12.7 cm) long and is deposited in a rough coils that are 8 to 10 inches (20 to 25 cm) across.

The color of grizzly scat may be bright red from wild raspberries, dark blue if the bear's recent diet has consisted primarily of blueberries, or dark brown to black from vegetable matter. The texture of the feces varies widely according to diet as well, from a tightly knit mass held together with hair (after a bear has dined on carrion) to a runny, semiliquid mass that results from eating a berry-rich diet.

Bear feces are often dark brown or black due to vegetative content. (Robert H. Busch)

TRACKS

In 1961, Adolph Murie wrote in *A Naturalist in Alaska* that "a bear track at any time may create a stronger emotion than the old bear himself, for the imagination is brought into play . . . the bear is somewhere, and he may be anywhere."

Grizzlies walk in what is called *plantigrade fashion,* meaning that they walk with the feet placed down flat. Dogs, on the other hand, are *digitigrade* walkers, meaning they walk on their toes, an adaption for improved running speed. Flat-footed species like bears are usually heavy and slow; although grizzlies can run fast over short distances, they rely on strength more than speed for survival.

The tracks of grizzlies are composed of huge hindpaw imprints and smaller forepaw prints. Because of the great weight of the grizzly, its tracks register in almost any medium. And because its claws are nonretractable, they almost always leave their awesome impression.

The hindfoot prints of the grizzly look incredibly like those of a human. Frederick Dellenbaugh, an artist with the 1871 and 1872 John Wesley Powell expeditions on the Colorado River, wrote in *A Canyon Voyage,* "I . . . was surprised to discover what I took to be the fresh print of the bare foot of a man . . . my companions laughed and warned me to be cautious . . . It was the track of a grizzly bear."

The hindprint of a big male grizzly may be 10 to 12 inches (25 to 30 cm) long and 6 inches (15 cm) wide. If a foot that size belonged to a human, it would take a size 20 shoe. The hindprints of a black bear

Grizzlies walk in plantigrade fashion, on the soles of the feet. (Robert H. Busch)

A grizzly's rear foot looks amazingly like that of a human. (Robert H. Busch)

are much smaller—they rarely exceed 6 inches by 4 inches (15 cm by 10 cm).

Each foot has five toes, but the "big toe" on a grizzly is the outermost toe (see photo), not the inner one as in humans. The little inside toe often does not leave a mark: A grizzly may leave a four-toed track instead of the normal five, which often confuses first-time trackers.

The front paw print of a grizzly is about 5¼ inches (13 cm) long and 5½ inches (14 cm) wide. The round heelpad of the front paw often does not register, except in very fine sand or mud.

One way to distinguish grizzly tracks from black bear tracks, aside from size, is the fact that in prints left by black bears, the claws leave marks about ½ inch (1.2 cm) in front of the toe pads, whereas grizzly

Grizzly tracks found near Mt. Robson, Alberta. (Jean Capps/ DragonSnaps)

The claws of a young grizzly are brown-black; with age, they will turn white. (B. C. Wildlife Branch)

claws, being much longer, leave impressions 1 to 2 inches (2.5 to 5.0 cm) in front. Although tall tales exist of grizzlies with 5-inch (13-cm) claws, the longest front claws that veteran grizzly biologist Stephen Herrero has ever seen measured exactly 3.87 inches (9.83 cm).

Grizzly toe prints tend to fall along nearly a straight line. Black bear toepad prints tend to be more separate and lie along a distinct curve.

When a grizzly is walking, there may be only a 4-inch (10-cm) stride between grizzly tracks, but when the big bear is running full out, the stride may stretch to as much as 45 inches (114 cm). A slow

Deep grizzly footprints in Khutzeymateen Provincial Park, British Columbia. (Dan Wakeman)

amble results in an abbreviated stride and pairs of tracks that almost register on top of each other. An all-out run results in a very long stride and a track with the front feet printing in pairs behind the back feet.

Many areas exist in both Alaska and British Columbia where the great bear has, over hundreds of years, worn deep trails. Along Lake Iliamna, Alaska, I have seen grizzly trails that look like wagon tracks—two deep parallel ruts about 2 feet (0.6 m) apart.

In the Khutzeymateen Valley of northwestern British Columbia, centuries of use have resulted in winding trails consisting of deep depressions in the mossy forest floor where hundreds of bears have trod precisely in old tracks. Occasionally, these tracks fill with water and seeds fall in, resulting in bizarre patches of grass that wander through the woods.

SENSES

Sight

One common bear myth is that grizzlies have poor eyesight. One reason for the myth is the size of a grizzly's eyes; compared to the huge dish-shaped face, the eyes look like two tiny raisins lost in a vast brown pudding. Actually, although grizzlies are nearsighted, their sight is quite good.

Contrary to popular belief, grizzlies do not have poor eyesight, although they rely more on smell than sight. (Robert H. Busch)

The grizzly's eyesight is similar in acuity to that of humans. (Robert H. Busch)

Naturalist John Craighead, who spent over a decade observing the grizzlies of Yellowstone National Park, believes that grizzlies can recognize objects at distances of almost 200 feet (60 m).

In one famous experiment in the 1930s, it was found that European brown bears—close relatives of the grizzly—could visually recognize humans who they know from over 300 feet (91 m) away.

Although grizzlies are attracted to colors, there has been little investigation into their ability to detect color. According to grizzly biologist Charles Jonkel, "color perception is usually an indication of a visually keen animal" (Domico, 1988).

Smell

When a grizzly rears on its hind legs and appears to peer around as if it were near-blind, it is actually just gaining a lofty viewpoint and a better chance at getting a good scent. According to University of Calgary grizzly expert Stephen Herrero (1985), "smell is the fundamental and most important sense a bear has."

According to a Native American legend, when a leaf fell in the forest, the eagle saw it fall, the coyote heard it fall, but the grizzly smelled it fall.

The grizzly's sense of smell is so acute that it can detect humans from up to 2 miles (about 3 km) away. (Robert H. Busch)

Although its sense of eyesight is similar to that of humans, a grizzly's sense of smell is far superior. Humans live in a world dominated by sight. Grizzlies live in a world dominated by smell.

In all mammals, one measure of the sense of smell is the area of the olfactory mucosa, the mucous membrane located in the nose. In

A grizzly's sense of smell is about 75 times as powerful as that of humans. (Robert H. Busch)

humans, the olfactory mucosa is usually less than a square inch (6 square cm) in area; in bears, it may be a hundred times larger.

Many anecdotes describe the grizzly's excellent sense of smell. Jim Stanton, who lived for 40 years in the remote Knight Inlet of western British Columbia, once observed a group of bears that clearly smelled a boatful of humans from a distance of 2 miles (3 km). And one old blind female in what is now Denali National Park in Alaska was known to have raised at least three generations of cubs with only the directions given to her by her nose and ears.

Hearing

Grizzlies have small ears that range from 1.2 to 3½ inches (3.0 to 3.6 cm) in length.

A grizzly's hearing, according to Stephen Herrero (1985), probably extends into the "ultrasonic range of 16 to 20 million hertz, perhaps higher." This makes the grizzly's hearing slightly better than that of humans, whose total hearing range extends from about 20- to 20,000 hertz.

A grizzly can often pick up the sounds of a human voice from a quarter-mile (⅓ km or so) away. The bear is often long gone before humans stumble into its area.

A grizzly's hearing ranges into higher frequencies than are audible to the human ear. (Robert H. Busch)

Touch

The grizzly has a sensitive touch, with especially sensitive lips and paws.

I have often watched grizzlies use their lips to pluck berries from a thorny branch with many more times the dexterity that I could. The front and rear footpads of a grizzly are also highly sensitive, and many reports exist of bears juggling stones or bits of wood in their front paws.

Grizzlies often use a single claw to remove eggs from a fish, a delicate operation for so large a predator. At McNeil River, Alaskan writer Tom Walker once saw "a bear try to shake the water out of its ears, then insert a single claw into its ear and gently scratch at the irritation" (Walker, 1993).

In 1964, when Alaska experienced the worst earthquake in its history, grizzlies were noticed heading for the hills prior to the event. Many biologists believe that the animals could detect the tiny tremors in the earth that preceded the big quake and left the lowlands as a result.

Grizzlies have a sensitive sense of touch, and can scratch one ear with amazing dexterity. (Robert McCaw)

Having a good scratch. (Robert H. Busch)

DISEASES AND PARASITES

Grizzlies suffer from more than 80 kinds of internal and external parasites, of which over half are internal worms such as hookworms, roundworms, and tapeworms.

Up to 50 percent of many bear populations suffer from trichinosis, caused by the tiny roundworm known as *Trichinella spiralis*.

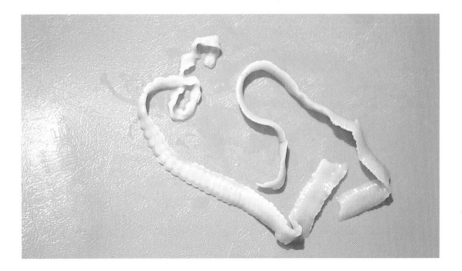

Tapeworms are a common parasite of many grizzlies. (Robert H. Busch)

41

Older bears can suffer from cataracts, arthritis, and a host of other maladies common to humans. (Jean Capps/DragonSnaps)

Bears inadvertently ingest the encysted *Trichinella* larvae when they eat fresh meat or carrion. The larvae then mature in the bear's intestinal tract, enter the bloodstream, and move through blood vessels to the muscles, causing pain, vomiting, and diarrhea. In acute infestations, death can arise from cardiac or respiratory failure. Up to 40 percent of humans who eat uncooked infected bear meat suffer the same symptoms and die.

External parasites include such pests as two genera of fleas and one tick species.

Diseases common to grizzlies include such common problems as arthritis and pneumonia, plus more exotic diseases such as tuberculosis, rabies, canine distemper, brucellosis, and leptospirosis. Grizzlies get tooth cavities and eye cataracts that are very similar to those in humans. They also can suffer from hemorrhoids.

LONGEVITY

Although there is one record of a captive grizzly living to the age of 47 in a zoo, most wild bears are lucky to reach 25. The oldest wild grizzly on record in Alaska was 35; the oldest one in British Columbia lived to age 34.

In captivity, grizzlies may live into their late forties; in the wild, rarely to 35. (Robert H. Busch)

Natural mortality among grizzlies is highest among cubs. Mortality among first-year cubs has been documented as high as 75 percent in northern Canada, with mortality for second-year cubs at 25 percent. These figures were documented by biologist John Nagy on Richards Island and the Tuktoyaktuk Peninsula of northern Canada, where food is scarce for the big bear. Biologist Arthur Pearson found

Young cubs are curious and incautious; many do not survive their first year. (Karl Sommerer)

This grizzly cub was killed by a truck when it tried to cross the highway near the British Columbia-Alberta border. (Jean Capps/DragonSnaps)

that in the southwest Yukon, 21 percent of cubs died in their first three years.

At the McNeil River bear sanctuary in Alaska, one study found that 40 percent of the cubs did not survive to the age of one and a half (Egbert and Luque, 1975).

Causative mortality factors for cub deaths include malnutrution, accidents, and predation by larger bears.

Larger bears, especially big males, are well-known cub-killers in some parts of the continent, although this factor is probably overestimated in the minds of the public. I once lived for four years in a remote part of central British Columbia, where each fall I watched a number of grizzlies gather to feed on spawning salmon. Despite thousands of hours of observations, I never saw an adult male kill a cub. And at the McNeil River State Game Sanctuary in Alaska, manager Larry Aumiller and his crew have only witnessed one such killing in 16 years.

That notable event occurred in 1991, when the salmon runs in southern Alaska were poor and the bears were very competitive for food. When two young cubs were left alone for a short while, a medium-sized male approached quickly, grabbed one of the cubs, and shook it by the back until it was dead. The bear then fed upon the unfortunate cub, leaving only the head and feet.

That killing was likely the result of insufficient food, but many other factors may account for adult males killing cubs. The predation may have some genetic benefit, for it may cause females to come into heat again, allowing the dominant males to breed and continue their genetic line.

Much of the predation, however, is probably incidental—merely the case of a hungry large bear viewing a small cub as a source of meat. Cases have even been reported of young cubs feeding upon their dead mother and of mother bears eating their dead cubs. In the world of the wild, there is little room for sentimentality.

Mortality is also high just after grizzlies emerge from their winter dens. At this time, there is usually still snow on the ground and the thin bears, whose layer of fat has been used up during hibernation, have a hard time finding enough to eat.

Subadults, because of a lack of experience, often have a high mortality rate. This is especially true of subadult males, which tend to have larger ranges and hence a larger chance of running into humans or human activities.

Natural deaths among adult bears can be due to a variety of causes. Of 12 female grizzlies known to have died from natural causes in the Rocky and Columbia Mountains of North America, 5 were killed by other bears, 3 died in rock or snow avalanches, 3 from unknown causes, and 1 in a collapsed den (McLellan et al., 1999).

When grizzlies emerge from the den, and snow is still on the ground, it is often difficult to find food. (Karl Sommerer)

Of greater impact on grizzly populations is the greatest predator of all—*Homo sapiens.* Studies abound that cite humans as the main reason for grizzly deaths. Of 639 known deaths of bears studied between 1993 and 1999 in Alberta's Eastern Slopes Grizzly Project, 627 were caused by humans. Ninety percent of known grizzly deaths in the Greater Yellowstone Ecosystem have been attributed to humans or human activities, mostly on private lands surrounding Yellowstone National Park. In another study of 95 grizzlies in Yellowstone National Park, one bear in three was dead seven years later. Eighty-four percent of the deaths were caused by humans. And in a 1999 summary (McLellan et al., 1999) that investigated the deaths of 388 radio-collared grizzlies between 1975 and 1997, humans were reported to have killed 77 to 85 percent of the known or suspected dead bears. This study also found that "without radiotelemetry, management agencies would have been unaware of about half (46 to 51 percent) of the deaths."

Total mortality, natural and human-caused, for bears 6 years of age or younger has been documented at 62 to 77 percent for Yellowstone bears (Knight and Eberhardt, 1984) and 65 percent for grizzlies in the northern Yukon (Nagy, unpublished data).

To put it more simply, most grizzlies never even make it to the age of 6, a sad fact of life for one of the most magnificent animals on the continent.

CHAPTER

3

Hungry as a Bear

. . . a lisson on the charcter
of the grissly Baare.

JAMES CLYMAN, 1824

HOME RANGE

Grizzlies are not truly territorial, but they do roam indistinctly defined home ranges in search of food. The only true territories in the grizzly's world are the choice feeding spots at salmon-spawning streams or garbage dumps, which may be defended with vigor.

Ranges vary from 2.6 to 2,200 square miles (6.7 to 5,698 square km) in area, depending on the availability of food and the nature of the terrain. Areas with rugged terrain and high habitat diversity tend to lead to small home ranges. Areas with low habitat diversity and a shortage of food items tend to lead to very large home ranges; the largest ranges on record for grizzlies are those along the Arctic coastal plains of Alaska, where food sources are few and far between (see Table 1).

Males tend to wander over larger territories than females. This is likely due to two factors. Firstly, a larger range enhances the chances of a male finding a female of breeding age. And secondly, because males tend to be larger and heavier, a larger range, all other things being equal, provides more food than a smaller range.

Grizzly home ranges overlap to some extent, which makes it easier for males and females to get together in the breeding season.

Sizes and boundries of home ranges are elastic, changing year after year with changes in food sources and habitat. One grizzly in the Northwest Territories of Canada had a home range that stretched from 26 square miles (68 square km) to 102 square miles (265

Table 1 Grizzly Home Ranges

Square Miles		Square Kilometers		Area	Source
2.6		6.7		Kodiak I., AK	1
36(M)	51(F)	92(M)	133(F)	Kananaskis, AB	2
249	84	644	217	Jasper, AB	3
419	94	1086	244	Swan Hills, AB	4
540	51	1398	133	Mission Mts., MT	5
1064	194	2755	502	Berland R., AB	6

Sources: 1 = Troyer & Hensel, 1969; 2 = Wielgus, 1986; 3 = Russell, 1979; 4 = Nagy & Russell, 1978; 5 = Servheen & Lee, 1979; 6 = Dood et al., 1986.

square km) because of changes in the availability of food (Miller and Tait, 1982).

Home ranges also change with changes in the family. As cubs mature, the size of maternal home ranges usually increases, so that females with cubs of the year often have smaller ranges than females with yearlings. Again, the larger range used by a female with older cubs presumably provides more food for the larger cubs, but may also relate to the increased ability of older cubs to travel a larger distance.

Finally, home ranges expand and contract with the seasons. Summer ranges tend to be larger because food sources are more scattered. Fall ranges tend to be smaller, as food sources such as spawning salmon or berry patches become concentrated in small areas.

I personally was able to document grizzly home ranges here in my home province of British Columbia. For four years, I lived at the north end of a remote lake, and nearby, grizzlies arrived each fall to feed on spawning salmon. Their home range in the fall was restricted to the small valley with the salmon stream. But as the middle of October approached, the bears wandered back into the mountains, where they would sleep in peace during the cruel Canadian winters. The bears were remarkably consistent: They always arrived in the second-to-last week of August, and they always left by the second week in October, in response to some inner clock to which I was not privy.

Some of the smallest home ranges on record for bears are on the various Alaskan islands, where rich diets of salmon and berries allow dense concentrations of grizzlies. In the Kodiak National Wildlife Refuge, on Alaska's Kodiak Island, there is a cozy density of 1 bear per 1½ square miles (3.9 square km). Densities elsewhere range up to 91 square miles (237 square km) per grizzly (see Table 2).

Bear densities often show the effect of human overharvesting. According to the 1990 *Management Plan for Grizzly Bears in Alberta,* "Densities of bears for the Alaskan population, which had been hunted for 15 years, were one-quarter to one-seventh of those reported for the unhunted northern Yukon bears."

When relocated, grizzlies usually try to return to their home territory. In October 1994, a grizzly was relocated from its territory near Hinton, Alberta, to a new spot some 600 miles (909 km) farther north. Almost a year later, the wayward bear was shot by a hunter near Dease Lake in northwest British Columbia, over 900 miles (1,364 km) away. "For whatever reason, his internal navigation sys-

Table 2 Grizzly Densities

Square Miles/Bear	Square Kilometers/Bear	Area	Source
0.6	1.5	Kodiak I., AK	1
4	11	Khutzeymateen, BC	2
8	21	Glacier NP, MT	3
10.5	27.2	S.W. Yukon	4
27–32	69–82	Kananaskis, AB	5
40–51	104–131	Swan Hills, AB	6
81	211–237	Arctic coastal plain	7

Sources: 1 = Troyer & Hensel, 1969; 2 = Nag & MacHutchon, 1991; 3 = Martinka, 1974; 4 = Pearson, 1975; 5 = Carr, 1989; 6 = Nagy & Russell, 1978; 7 = Nagy, 1983.

tem went haywire and he probably thought he was heading home," says Tony Hamilton, a bear biologist in British Columbia.

Another grizzly was recently relocated 100 miles (150 km) from the Pemberton Valley of southern British Columbia to the northern Cascade Mountains. One month later, the bear was shot back in his old digs. Matt Austin, carnivore specialist for the B.C. Wildlife

Grizzlies will often rest during the day in shallow beds such as this one dug in a cool patch of dirt and sand. (Robert H. Busch)

Shaking the water free after a refreshing dip in an Alaskan stream. (Karl Sommerer)

Branch, was amazed at the bear's travels. "He made his way across the TransCanada Highway, across the Fraser River and all the human and natural barriers in between, to reach the Pemberton Valley," Austin says. "It would have been very interesting to see exactly how he did it" (quoted in Pynn, 1999).

HIBERNATION

According to a native American legend, the beaver taught humankind how to build houses, the heron how to spear fish, and the coyote how to hunt. But before the bear could teach humans how to sleep through the winter, a hunter killed one of them, and as a result, humans were forever condemned to suffer through the long cold winter.

The fall is a desperate time for grizzlies, as they become literally "hungry as a bear." Grizzlies must eat prodigious amounts of food totalling up to 40,000 calories per day, resulting in a weight gain of 5 or 6 pounds (2.3 to 2.7 kg) a day, in preparation for winter hibernation. By late fall, a grizzly's weight may be 85 percent higher than it was in the previous spring. One big male on Alaska's Kodiak Island put on 205 pounds (93 kg) in 70 days during one fall season.

This grizzly in Denali National Park is foraging many hours a day prior to hibernation. (Karl Sommerer)

During the fall, the fur on grizzlies' backs grows thick, which provides extra insulation during the long sleep, and a fat layer up to 10 inches (25 cm) thick is laid down.

Late October and November are the times when most grizzlies start seeking out a den in which to hibernate over the winter.

Technically, grizzlies are not true hibernators. True hibernation is a complex winter survival mechanism that has been most intensively studied in the ground squirrel. During the ground squirrel's hibernation, its heart rate is reduced drastically, from 500 beats to about 25 beats a minute; its lungs take in only 2 percent of the air the squirrel normally needs; its body metabolism drops to $\frac{1}{25}$ of its normal rate; and its body temperature plunges to within a few degrees of freezing.

With grizzlies, however, the heart rate decreases to 8 to 12 beats a minute from the normal 40 to 70 beats per minute, the metabolic rate drops by a half, and the body temperature drops only a few degrees from a normal 98.5° to 99°F (36.9° to 37.2°C) to 89° to 90°F (31.7° to 32.2°C).

Researchers have found that the ground squirrel's plunge into hibernation is determined by genes. One gene produces an enzyme that helps the squirrels burn their stored fat. Another helps the blood stay fluid during extremely cold temperatures. One gene keeps the body

Bears must pack on the pounds prior to hibernation in order to survive the long cold winter. (Robert H. Busch)

from using up its stores of glucose. (Glucose is fuel for the brain, and as such, is crucial to the squirrel's survival.) And yet another gene prevents the blood from clotting as the squirrels hibernate.

It is not known if grizzlies possess genes with similar functions, but the matter is a subject of great research. If humans could be placed into a similar deep sleep, they might better survive extreme cold or oxygen deprivation, and be able to emerge from comas with few ill effects. Organs harvested for transplants might also stay viable longer. And for extended travel into deep space, nothing would be more fitting than a deep sleep along the way. The last Mars probe, for example, took nearly a year to reach the red planet; if humans had been along for the ride, their long ride would have been facilitated by a deep hibernation.

During the period of hibernation, grizzlies do not normally eat or drink, but they are adapted to survive through an elegant series of physiological changes:

- ◆ Body fats and carbohydrates are broken down to form water, which helps prevent the bear from dehydrating.

- ◆ A small amount of muscle protein is broken down to produce urea, which is then recycled to make more protein, reducing the need for food during this period of rest.

♦ Muscle protein is also broken down to produce glucose, which is essential for vital brain functions in grizzlies as well as squirrels.

♦ During hibernation, the kidneys of a grizzly remove urea from the blood, which again is recycled into protein.

All of these functions provide nutrients for sleeping grizzlies. As an Abenaki native saying goes, "A bear is wiser than man, because a man does not know how to live all winter without eating anything."

One of the many mysteries of hibernation is why hibernating grizzlies don't suffer from high cholesterol, after drawing heavily upon their own fat reserves all winter.

Bears without sufficient fat reserves may leave their hibernation dens to find food. (Fernandez & Peck/Adventure Photo & Film)

Bears that enter hibernation without sufficient fat reserves may leave the den and search for additional food. Bears that do this are often subadults with little experience at life in the wild.

Some of these bears became the Inuit's dreaded "winter bear," or "ice bear." Wandering bears sometimes find a patch of open water or slush, and by either rolling in it or walking through it, their fur gets wet. The fur then freezes, creating a bear clad in an armor of ice. Legends grew about bears whose coats could stop arrows and spears, and the feared "ice bear" became part of Inuit mythology.

Today, winter loggers and snowmobilers are increasingly causing problems by disturbing hibernating grizzlies. An awakened grizzly may not return to its den, and unless it can dig another one, it may die.

One grizzly disturbed from its den near Rogers Peak in British Columbia didn't bother to dig a new den at all. A park ranger found the bear curled up under a mound of snow on an abandoned spur of the Canadian Pacific Railway. The bear lay there undisturbed until April, when it awoke and ambled away from the unusual den site.

Most dens are situated to ensure early snow cover and tend to be at high elevations, ranging from 3,000 to 10,000 feet (915 to 3049 m). Sixty-one percent of grizzly dens in Yellowstone National Park are on northern slopes, at elevations between 6,500 feet and 10,000 feet (1,982 to 3,049 m); most are in the 8,000-foot to 9,000-foot (2439-m to 2744-m) range.

Dens are often dug under large rocks or tree roots, with an entrance that is just large enough to admit the bear. Almost exactly half of the dens in Yellowstone National Park are under large trees, with a network of roots that provide a supportive roof for the underground den. Grizzlies on Alaska's Unimak Island occasionally den up in long natural tunnels in lava beds.

Grizzlies may travel up to 30 miles (45 km) just to seek a fitting den site. Occasionally they reuse old dens, but more often they dig new ones in the same general area.

The average grizzly den is a small structure not much larger than the bear itself, measuring about 6½ feet (2 m) long, 4½ feet (1.4 m) wide, and 3 feet (0.9 m) high.

There are exceptions, however. One ambitious Alaskan bear once dug a den a total of 19 feet (5.8 m) long, with a comfy 6-foot by 9-foot (1.8-m by 2.7-m) chamber at the end.

The denning chamber is often elevated, providing both a heat trap and good drainage if the den's roof should leak. Dens may be lined with grass or soft tree boughs, sometimes to a depth of about 10 inches (25 cm).

Pregnant females are usually the first to den up, followed by lone females, females with young, and then subadults and adult males. When the bears emerge from the den, the reverse order is often the case.

Just what arouses grizzlies and other animals from hibernation is a matter of some dispute. It is known that there is a spontaneous liberation of heat from stored fat, accompanied by a rapid acceleration of the heart rate. But what triggers these physiological changes is not known.

Upon emerging from the den, grizzlies often spend a week or two in the vicinity of the den. The time of emergence is likely keyed to a number of factors, including length of day, temperature, barometric pressure, and depth of snow over the den. Some grizzlies are remarkably constant in their dates of emergence; one old male in the Knight Inlet area of western British Columbia emerged on the same day (April 15) for eight years (Day, 1994).

By the end of hibernation, half of the bear's weight may have been devoured by the bear's metabolic needs. An adult grizzly may burn up 4,000 to 8,000 calories per day during hibernation. Yellowstone National Park grizzlies lose between 8 and 18 percent of their fall weight during hibernation. In northern Canaada, the percentage

Female bears, along with their young, usually den up before male bears do. (Kennan Ward/Adventure Photo & Film)

varies between 24 and 43 percent. Bears that do not gain sufficient weight during the fall often die during winter.

The first scat passed by the bear after emergence is often long and dry. One bear scat found in Alaska measured an amazing 29½ inches (74.9 cm) long by 2 inches (5.1 cm) wide. These scats have led to tales of bears using fecal plugs to plug up their anuses prior to hibernation. The truth, however, is simply that the lack of water and lack of movement during hibernation causes the dry scat, a condition that often occurs with bed-ridden humans.

Toward the end of hibernation, a pregnant female grizzly will temporarily awaken to give birth, and the marvelous cycle of life begins again.

REPRODUCTION

Through most of the year, grizzlies are loners, ambling quietly through their home ranges in search of food. In late spring to early summer, however, males feel the urge for female company. In my home province of British Columbia, most grizzly matings take place in June, but across the rest of the continent, matings may occur anytime from April through July. There are also a few records from

Grizzlies are one of the slowest-reproducing of all mammals, a factor that (combined with habitat loss) has led to their decimation across North America. (Mark Newman/Adventure Photo & Film)

southern Alaska of matings in August. The female grizzly is in estrus—the prime receptive heat period—for 16 to 27 days.

Females advertise their readiness to breed through an enlarged vulva and the release of sex hormones in urine and feces. Sexually aroused males may walk with a noted swagger, salivate copiously, and urinate on their own bellies and legs. Mated couples may play together, gently bite each other, nuzzle each other, and frequently smell each other's genital region prior to copulation.

Each male may breed with more than one female. There is one record of a Yellowstone National Park grizzly mating ten times with four males in two hours, making the action in most human singles bars look incredibly tame in comparison.

The bears stay physically coupled for up to 45 minutes. Male grizzlies achieve erections not through blood engorgement, as in humans, but with a bony structure in the penis called a baculum, which may reach 7 inches (20 cm) in length.

The male bear takes the top position, grasping the female with his front legs and sometimes biting her neck. If he becomes too aggressive, the female will often reach around and bite him. Occasionally the female seems to lose interest halfway through the mating and begins to amble off or even begin grazing. I have often seen females

Mating grizzlies may stay physically coupled for up to half an hour or more. (Karl Sommerer)

After copulating with her mate, this female grizzly in Alaska is growling a warning to another male grizzly. (Karl Sommerer)

start to walk away with their mates still hanging on for dear life. The males rarely stay with their mates for more than a few days, and play no role in raising the young.

Some males, however, are quite possessive and try gamely to keep "their" females in restricted areas to prevent them from mating with other bears. This type of herding behavior has been noted in both Banff National Park in Alberta and Denali National Park in Alaska. In a 1977 study in Banff National Park, University of Calgary biologist Stephen Herrero found one ardent male who kept a female confined to a 5- to 8-acre (1- to 3-hectare) area for 13 days during the breeding season.

Males will also fight with other males over females, and many old male grizzlies have deep scars on their muzzles from such encounters. When challenging another male, grizzlies often use what has been termed a "cowboy walk," in which they walk on stiff bowlegs toward each other with lowered head and angry intentions. The posing often deters a fight before it begins, but when an actual tussle occurs, serious injuries can occur.

Occasionally, the fights are fatal. The autopsy of one such unfortunate bear, who obviously lost in his fight, revealed 89 puncture wounds, a wide hole in the chest, broken ribs, a broken shoulder, a broken nose, a dislocated neck, and a broken skull. Those males who survive such battles pass on their genes to the next generation.

The big male in the foreground is chasing away a rival over the affections of a female. (Karl Sommerer)

The grizzly's gestation period is about 235 days. A mother grizzly displays *delayed implantation,* in which a new embryo (blastocyst) floats freely for months before finally attaching itself to the uterine wall to grow and develop. This allows female grizzlies to fatten up by themselves in the fall without having to tend to pesky cubs. Once the

These two subadults are watching a mating pair of bears with great interest. (Karl Sommerer)

Cubs stay close to their mother for at least the first 2 years of life. (Karl Sommerer)

cubs are born, the female's body is well equipped to handle their heavy nutritional demands. It also allows the cubs to emerge into the big wild world at the optimal time of the year—early spring—when abundant fresh food is available.

Delayed implantation is delicately tuned to the female's health and overall condition. Usually there are three to five blastocysts floating in the female's womb. If the female has entered the den in poor condition, none of the embryos will implant in the uterine wall, so that all of her resources can be used to keep herself alive during hibernation. If she is in good condition, two or three blastocysts may implant.

Females in extremely poor condition may not conceive at all, or may conceive and then die. There is one record of a radio-collared Yellowstone National Park mother bear who died in her den from malnutrition and was fed upon by her cubs.

Female grizzlies are not sexually mature until 4 to 8 years of age; males are not sexually mature until 5 to 10 years of age. If an adult bear can survive the many rigors of life in the wild, it can be sexually active for many years; one Yellowstone female grizzly gave birth at the age of 26 and a Flathead Valley, Montana, female gave birth at the age of 27.

Females sometimes breed every other year, but they often breed only every three or four years. The grizzly is thus the slowest repro-

Although twins are more common, triplets among grizzlies are not unusual. (Karl Sommerer)

ducing of all the great predators in North America. One female grizzly will often only raise one or two female offspring to adulthood during her entire life. According to the World Wildlife Fund, "the removal of even a single grizzly can have a serious biological impact on a particular bear population." Unfortunately, far too many government wildlife branches were late in recognizing this important factor in grizzly management.

Grizzly cubs are born in late winter through early spring, typically around late January. A grizzly's first litter is often just a single cub, but later litters may range from one to four cubs; the average litter is two cubs. There is one record of a Canadian grizzly that had six cubs.

Biologists divide animals into one of two groups, depending upon reproductive strategies. Species such as turtles and rabbits are classed as *r-selected* species. These species produce huge numbers of young in the hope that at least one or two will survive to adulthood to perpetuate the species.

Grizzlies, on the other hand, are *K-selected,* meaning that they produce very few young, but guard and raise them carefully, so that as many as possible will reach sexual maturity.

At birth, grizzly cubs weigh only about 1 pound (0.4 kg) and are about 9 inches (23 cm) long. Their birth weight is about $\frac{1}{300}$ to $\frac{1}{500}$ of the weight of the mother bear. A human baby typically weighs about $\frac{1}{15}$ the weight of its mother.

A female grizzly often nurses in a prone position, with one cub on each side. (Karl Sommerer)

The tiny grizzly cubs are so poorly developed at birth that an old folk belief stated that cubs were born as mere amorphous lumps of flesh, which were then licked into bear shape by their mothers. This is the origin of the expression "licked into shape," still widely used today. In France, mothers call naughty children "badly licked bears."

The cubs are born toothless and blind. Their eyes open at about 21 days, and the little bears are fully weaned by about 24 weeks.

Young cubs grow quickly on their mother's milk, which is ten times richer than cow's milk. Grizzly milk averages about 33 percent fat, 11 percent protein, and about 10 percent carbohydrate, yielding 41 to 88 kilocalories per ounce (6 to 13 kilojoules per gram). The cubs typically nurse for about 10 minutes every 2 or 3 hours. They often emit a low, gurgling sound as they suckle.

The female usually nurses the cubs while she is sitting upright like some giant hairy Buddha, or lying prone on the ground. A female grizzly may burn 4,000 kilocalories (16,597 kilojoules) a day just nursing her cubs.

Cubs often nurse at times of stress, such as when big male grizzlies are in the area, or after they have a bad scare from some other experience. When the mother decides that her cubs have fed enough, she unceremoniously stands up, sending her young ones tumbling to the ground.

This cub isn't letting any space get between himself and his mother. (Karl Sommerer)

Female grizzlies have six nipples, four on the chest and two on the lower abdomen. Polar bears, which have smaller litters, have only four nipples.

It is not unusual for cubs to choose a favorite nipple for feeding. White, a large female who was well known to researchers at Alaska's McNeil River State Game Sanctuary, once had three cubs, one of whom died over a winter. Each of the two remaining cubs chose a favorite feeding station.

Larry Aumiller, sanctuary manager, recounts their feeding strategy: "The light one almost always nursed on White's right side, the dark one on her left. Twenty-one out of 24 times, they were on their favorite sides" (Walker, 1993).

When the cubs leave the den, sometime between April and June, they typically weigh about 5 to 6 pounds (2.3 to 2.7 kg). Two months later, they may weigh 10 times as much. Cubs often nurse into their second summer and occasionally into their third.

The mother and cubs usually stay around the den site for a couple of weeks after emerging in the early spring. Before ranging far from the den, the cubs gain in strength and size, all under the watchful eye of their mother. There is some evidence that mothers and cubs who move down to lower elevations immediately after emerging from the den suffer higher mortality rates (primarily from attacks by

Play is an important mechanism for testing strength, establishing dominance, and forging bonds between siblings. (Robert H. Busch)

adult bears) than those who stay around the den site. Newborn cubs are so small and helpless that it is much safer for them to gain strength and experience in a known environment.

In situations where there is abundant food, such as at the salmon spawning grounds on Alaska's McNeil River, females may actually share the duties of raising cubs. Two McNeil grizzlies, with eight cubs between them, are known to have taken turns nursing the cubs and leading them to the fishing grounds. Goldie, a big McNeil female, was once observed nursing nine cubs at once from three different litters. Biologist L. P. Glenn documented three McNeil females, each with three cubs, who socialized closely with each other and exchanged cubs almost daily.

Much of the cubs' daily activities consist of three things—play, play, and more play. Cubs wrestle with each other, chase each other, play tug-of-war, juggle sticks and stones, and generally drive their poor mothers to distraction.

Play serves a number of useful purposes, including strengthening bonds between siblings, providing a means of exercise, testing

Young grizzlies, such as this subadult, spend much of their time playing. (Robert H. Busch)

Open mouths are often a sign of play, as seen here in these 2-year-old cubs. (Robert McCaw)

A cool river is a great place to play away an afternoon. (Karl Sommerer)

strength, establishing social dominance, and teaching survival skills that will be needed in the years to come.

Grizzlies generally play only with partners of equal size, one way to reduce serious injuries. Larry Aumiller, sanctuary manager at Alaska's McNeil River State Game Sanctuary, has watched many instances of grizzlies at play. "A bear that does involve itself in play with a bigger bear is often easily agitated and will break off the bout," he says. "Sometimes the smaller bear must react quite aggressively and forcefully to break off the encounter" (quoted in Walker, 1993). For the same reason, bears that are older than young cubs often play only with partners of the same sex.

Play time tends to diminish with age, but there are many records of adult bears sliding down snowbanks and then returning to the top of the slope to do it all again, apparently just for the fun of it.

In many areas, a healthy, well-fed bear is a happy, playful bear. Larry Aumiller says that "early in the season [at McNeil River] we see very little play, and later on, after the bears are sated on fish, there's a great deal of play" (quoted in Walker, 1993). Aumiller has observed play in bears as old as 18, unusual behavior that is likely related to the abundance of food in the sanctuary. Similarly, McNeil River is one of the few places in the world where a maternal female has been observed playing with an adult male.

These two cubs, ever curious, have discovered a new toy—a fishing float washed up on the beach. (Karl Sommerer)

The period from 6 months to 2½ years of age is a period of very rapid growth for grizzly cubs. After that, the rate of growth slows down. Females do not usually reach their maximum size until the age of 4 or 5 years; males until the age of 6 to 8.

A tree branch becomes a toy in the jaws of young grizzlies. (Robert H. Busch)

This grizzly family in southern Alaska is piled on a beach, enjoying the sunshine. (Karl Sommerer)

Young cubs stay with their mother for 1 to 3 years, learning the secrets of life in the wild and often imitating her behavior, body language, and feeding strategies. After this period, female cubs tend to disperse and establish their own home ranges within or near their mothers' home ranges. Subadult males, however, tend to disperse widely and establish their own ranges farther away.

The safest place in the world—tight behind a female grizzly. (Karl Sommerer)

Usually the dispersal process is instigated by the mother bear, and appears to be hormone-related. One piece of evidence for this is that one bear at McNeil River, who forcefully drove off her cubs when she entered her heat period, actually reunited with them when her cycle was over. A breeding female will chase and even bite her young to force them away when she comes into heat.

Orphaned cubs often die, but strong individuals may stay together for the sake of survival. Two orphaned cubs in Alberta's Jasper National Park in 1975 stayed together for almost four years before researchers lost track of them.

FOOD

In 1983, biologists David Hamer and Stephen Herrero conducted a study for Parks Canada in Alberta's Banff National Park and determined that about 80 percent of the diet of grizzlies in that park was plant material. A similar study in Glacier National Park yielded a similar result—a diet of 89 percent plant material. Grizzlies in Yellowstone National Park, on the other hand, are more carnivorous, eating a large number of bison and elk carcasses and fishing for spawning cutthroat trout.

A tough wall of cellulose surrounds internal nutrients in plants, which is why many herbivores (plant-eaters) have evolved large, multichambered stomachs and long digestive tracts in order to break down the cellulose. Grizzlies have a single-chambered stomach and a relatively short digestive tract for their size: The total length of the small intestine is usually between 28 and 29 feet (8.5 m and 9 m). This makes them inefficient plant-eaters, although their small intestine is longer than that of pure carnivores. In addition, food passes through the grizzly's digestive system quite quickly, adding to their apparent constant hunger.

The grizzly's life is thus one long search for food. As John Muir wrote in *Our National Parks*, "To him almost everything is food except granite."

The list of grizzly food items is a long one, including grass, sedges, bulbs, berries, bark, rodents, birds, insects, and fish. The grizzly's menu includes over 200 plant species alone, including such favorites as cow parsnip, skunk cabbage, glacier lily, devil's club, and

Young bears grow quickly on rich foods such as these lush sedges. (Karl Sommerer)

A grizzly may forage for vegetation for about 16 hours a day. (Robert H. Busch)

Devil's club, despite its thorns, is a favorite grizzly food. (Robert H. Busch)

horsetails. The list also includes items such as fungi and lichens, which, though less tasty, are rich in nutritional value.

Many of the grizzly's favorite plants are surprisingly rich in protein: cow parsnip (*Heracleum lanatum*) is 26 percent protein and 6.6 percent fat. Spring beauty (*Claytonia lanceolata*) is 29 percent protein and 3.8 percent fat. Even the lowly sedges can reach 26 percent in protein content by late June and July.

So dependent are most grizzlies on plants that many have been named after bears, including bearberry, bear grass, bear clover, bear wood, bear's grape, and bear huckleberry.

A grizzly may forage for up to 16 hours per day, resting only during the heat of midday in "daybeds," which are shallow beds scooped out of the earth that hold the big bear comfortably while it sleeps. A bear may have several daybeds within its feeding area, and tends to use whichever bed is closest. A typical daybed is about 6 to 8 feet (1.8 to 2.4 m) long, 5 or 6 feet (1.5 to 1.8 m) wide, and 1 to 3 feet (0.3 to 1 m) deep.

Peak periods of feeding are usually the crepuscular hours around dawn and dusk—from 6:00 A.M. to 7:00 A.M., and from 7:00 P.M. to around midnight during the extended twilight hours of summer in the Arctic.

Many of the bear's menu items are seasonal. Bears in the central Rockies often dine on roots in the spring, bistort and yampa in

A female grizzly and her two first-year cubs feeding on blueberries in Denali National Park. (Karl Sommerer)

the summer, berries in the middle and late summer, and pine nuts in the fall.

In early spring, carcasses of winter-killed deer, moose, and caribou are scavenged with great success. In late fall, the big bears are not above raiding squirrel caches for nuts and seeds.

In Yellowstone National Park, squirrel caches of whitebark pine cones provide a significant proportion of the grizzlies' diet. Whitebark pines grow at elevations above 8,000 feet (2,439 m) in Yellowstone National Park, making them one of the few rich food sources in the high alpine areas.

Pine cones may not seem very substantial as bear food, but some squirrel caches reach amazing sizes; biologists found one cache that contained almost 3,000 cones. The nuts within the cones are a rich source of food, averaging 78 percent oil. Grizzlies are able to locate pine-cone caches under as much as 6 feet (1.8 m) of snow by smell.

Almost all bears love carrion, but individual bears sometimes develop highly individual food preferences. One Yellowstone grizzly preferred to kill live elk, disdaining the numerous elk carcasses available to it.

Another grizzly's kill was once witnessed by a Yellowstone park ranger. The bear had surprised a herd of elk crossing the Madison River and killed one of the cows with a single mighty blow to its head with a front paw. The adult elk was killed instantly, the ranger said, in

Fat marmots are an important fall food source for many grizzlies (Robert H. Busch)

"an explosion of brains, blood, and bone fragments." Young fawns and calves are more common grizzly fare.

However, biologist Charles Jonkel, who has studied black bears, polar bears, and grizzlies, and has extensive experience comparing the three bruins, says that grizzlies are not adept at hunting. "Most

A big female teaches her two second-year cubs to fish in Alaska; cubs often grow up using exactly the same fishing techniques as their mothers. (Karl Sommerer)

This grizzly is trying to get a fish-eye view of his supper. (Karl Sommerer)

grizzly bears don't even know how to catch elk, deer, and such. They can become very good predators of those animals, but most of them don't have the foggiest idea how to do it," Jonkel says (quoted in Hummel, 1991).

Meat, either fresh on the hoof or as carrion, is often cached, to hide it from other scavengers. One such cache by a male grizzly was

Even this tough salmon is no match for a grizzly's mighty claws and jaws. (Karl Sommerer)

A careful spacing of bears prevents bloodshed along this salmon stream. (Karl Sommerer)

found by Alberta biologist Charles Mamo just outside the town of Banff. "[The grizzly had] found this drowned bull elk that fall and staked his claim," says Mamo. "He covered it over with debris and then lay on top of it, his paws dangling over the pile. Every once in a while, he would scoop down into the cache and eat some of it" (quoted in Turbak, 1984).

There are relatively few studies into the prey efficiency of the grizzly, or the percentage of prey chased by bears that is actually captured. One such study was undertaken in 1993 and 1994 by biologists Donald D. Young, Jr., and Thomas R. McCabe, who studied predation on the Porcupine caribou herd in northeastern Alaska. They found that only 28 percent of 32 caribou-bear encounters resulted in a kill. This statistic is only slightly higher than the 26-

Spawning sockeye salmon, a favorite grizzly food in many areas each fall. (Robert H. Busch)

percent prey efficiency documented by famed biologist George Schaller in his studies of lion-gazelle encounters in Tanzania.

Young and McCabe found that sows with young killed caribou more often than other bears, a finding that echoes researcher Steve French's findings in Yellowstone National Park that nearly a third of elk kills involved sows with young. This is almost to be expected, as sows with young are the grizzlies expected to have the highest food requirements.

Grizzlies preying on the caribou herd were found to kill few caribou calves older than 2 weeks of age. Young and McCabe estimated that grizzlies took about 2,000 caribou calves per year, representing about 5 to 7 percent of the estimated 43,000 calves produced annually by the Porcupine caribou herd.

A few unusual items appear on the grizzly's menu on occasion. For example, there is at least one documented account of a grizzly eating seals in the far north. In 1974, five grizzlies quickly found and feasted on a beached whale carcass on the south coast of Alaska. And in 1986, five grizzlies gathered at the Anderson River delta in Canada's Northwest Territories and devoured over 3,000 snow geese, plus thousands of eggs.

Grizzly fishing
techniques vary: Some
bears stand in one spot
and wait for supper to
swim by, some dive
after it, and some
snatch leaping salmon
right out of the air.
(Karl Sommerer)

(Mark Newman/
Adventure Photo & Film)

This subadult is intensely watching fish in the stream below him. (Robert H. Busch)

In the 1960s, naturalist Andy Russell documented another bizarre grizzly food item—ladybugs. Biologist Arthur Pearson documented a July diet rich in wasps in his study of grizzlies in the southwest Yukon.

Grizzlies in Alaska have been observed digging out clams. The bears detected the slimy seafood by either seeing the squirt of water

A plunge after a fish and success in Fish Creek, Alaska. (Jean Capps/DragonSnaps) (continued on next page)

Twin cubs fishing in Fish Creek, Alaska. (Jean Capps/DragonSnaps)

emitted by a clam or even hearing the spurt under the beach sand. Author Timothy Treadwell once watched a young Alaskan grizzly dig out and consume 67 clams in just over 2 hours. Grizzlies in British Columbia's Khutzeymateen Valley similarly often dine on mussels and barnacles.

At low tide, grizzlies forage for nutritious sedges, clams, barnacles, and mussels. (Karl Sommerer)

Ants, a favorite grizzly food item in many parts of the Rocky Mountains, may provide valuable amino acids.

Another unusual food item for grizzlies is army cutworm moths, which occur at elevations above 10,000 feet (3,049 m) in the Yellowstone area. The moths are highly nutritious, averaging 72 percent fat and 28 percent protein. One bear may gorge itself on over 20,000 moths a day. The moths emerge at night to feed on flower nectar, just the time when hungry grizzlies are foraging for food.

As Thomas McNamee wrote in *The Grizzly Bear* (1984), "They will eat some of the lowliest crud in the world, but they still know a square meal when it comes along."

Bears may also know a medicinal plant when it comes along. Many animal species, such as chimpanzees and gorillas, use various plants to ease intestinal upsets or to rid themselves of parasites. Bears may do this as well. At one time, the Navajo of the American Southwest learned from the grizzly to use plants of the lovage family to get rid of parasites. Grizzlies, observed the Navajo, chewed the roots of the plants, and then rubbed them into their fur as a natural remedy.

Unfortunately, many grizzlies have learned to love garbage. Undoubtedly, the most famous of garbage-habituated bears were the grizzlies in Yellowstone National Park. Grizzlies fed at Yellowstone Park dumps as early as the 1890s, and the park's first nuisance bears were identified by the early 1900s. By the 1930s, at least 260 individual bears were using the garbage dumps. The dumps were finally closed down in 1971.

In Alberta's Banff National Park, grizzlies regularly used to travel 25 miles (38 km) to feed upon garbage.

Across most of British Columbia, local dumps in rural areas are neither fenced nor utilize bear-proof containers, setting the stage for a disaster waiting to happen. Most garbage-eating bears end up shot by panicky humans who "don't want bears hanging around." As the B. C. Department of Environment, Lands and Parks says, "a fed bear is a dead bear."

Garbage-habituated bears are a group unto themselves, with very distinctive characteristics. Compared to bears that do not depend upon garbage, garbage-feeders tend to be heavier, have smaller home ranges, mature earlier, have larger litters, and breed more often than bears that stay away from garbage dumps.

Gulls are one of the many species that benefit from grizzly leftovers. (Karl Sommerer)

Berries play a major role in the diets of many grizzlies, and the bruins in turn play a major role in seed dispersal. Biologist Barrie Gilbert studied the relationship in Alaska's Katmai National Park and found that a big bear could excrete 400,000 berry seeds a day, spreading them over a wide area. Arthur Pearson, who studied grizzlies in the southwest Yukon, found that the average bear scat there contained an amazing 20,000 soapberry seeds.

Another study, by biologist R. D. Applegate, looked at the germination of cow parsnip seeds and found the rate was 16 percent higher in grizzly bear droppings than in seeds that fell directly from the plant.

Bears also play an important role in providing leftovers for a wide variety of smaller animals and birds, such as eagles, gulls, foxes, and coyotes. And as diggers extraordinaire, grizzlies open new ground for plants to colonize.

University of Victoria biologists have also found that grizzlies play an important role in fertilizing riparian plant growth. They have found grizzly-hauled salmon up to 492 feet (150 m) away from streams and have found amounts of salmon left on the forest floor equivalent to 3,563 pounds of commercial fertilizer per acre (4,195 kg per hectare). Much of the impressive tree growth alongside salmon streams is thus caused by the bears themselves, a remarkable and little-known achievement by a remarkable animal.

A mother grizzly, two cubs, and bald eagles— an impressive gathering of predators along a beach in Alaska. (Karl Sommerer)

INTERACTIONS WITH WOLVES AND COUGARS

In their endless pursuit of food, grizzlies often compete with the only other widely ranging carnivores on the continent, the wolf and the cougar.

Interesting observations on this topic have been recorded by Steve French. While French was a surgical resident at the University of

The wolf and the grizzly often compete for the same foods. (Robert H. Busch)

Grizzlies have been documented stealing food from another major predator, the cougar. (Robert H. Busch)

Utah in the late 1970s, he participated in the surgical work on a biologist who had been mauled by a grizzly at Yellowstone. The incident ignited his interest, and French has been researching the big bear ever since. He once monitored 113 cougar kills in Glacier and Yellowstone National Parks and found that grizzlies visited about a quarter of the cougar kills, robbing cougars of up to 26 percent of their food.

There are also many reports of grizzlies stealing food from wolf packs and of single grizzlies successfully defending their own food from a pack of wolves. In 1996, French watched one 350-pound (159-kg) grizzly chase nine wolves off an elk carcass and take possession of the prize.

Sometimes, however, the relationship between the two species is more amicable. French once watched two yearling grizzly cubs and three yearling wolf cubs playing together while the parents all watched, with no aggression from any party. Two of the young wolves even traveled and hunted with the bears for two days, proving that tolerance between species is possible, even in the vicious world of the predator.

COMMUNICATION AND SOCIAL STRUCTURE

Grizzlies communicate vocally through a large repertoire of woofs, whines, hums, growls, roars, and grunts and groans.

Grizzlies communicate primarily through body language, including facial expressions. (Robert H. Busch)

Because the great bear evolved in the treeless tundra, where there is good visibility over a long distance, grizzlies also depend heavily upon visual cues such as body language. Black bears tend to be more vocal.

Grizzlies who face you head on with flattened ears and a low stance are definitely bears to avoid. A bear who turns his head sideways is indicating submission.

To show submission, a grizzly turns its head to the side and slowly ambles away. (Robert H. Busch)

Bear scratches on trees may help in spacing bears apart or in attracting females through deposition of hormones on the tree. (Robert H. Busch)

Other forms of communication include the deposition of feces and scratching of trees.

Feces may contain traces of sex hormones called pheromones which indicate the breeding state of the animal.

Scratches on trees may be used as an avoidance mechanism, especially among male grizzlies; a way to advertise a bear's presence; a means of orientation, in the same way as humans use trail signs; or to promote estrus in females, through deposition of the male odor left on the tree.

Through vocal communication, body language, and tree scratches, grizzlies successfully avoid vicious battles that would result in serious injuries or even death. Biologists Allan Egbert and Michael Luque, who studied the big coastal grizzlies at Alaska's McNeil River in the 1970s, found that only 124 of more than 4,000 bear interactions they observed involved striking or biting.

Although the grizzly is usually a loner, some quite sociable behavior has been noted on occasion.

Biologist Rob Wielgus, who studied grizzlies in Alberta's Kananaskis Country northwest of Calgary between 1975 and 1985, once documented a close relationship among a female grizzly, her mother, and her daughters; the three generations of females got together and traveled together for a week or two. "They all lived in different home ranges, but adjacent to one another's," says Wielgus.

A serious fight over a fishing spot at McNeil Falls, Alaska. (Karl Sommerer)

"The daughter with the new cub traveled into her sister's home range, picked up her sister, and then the three of them traveled back to the 'grandmother' and met with her and her yearling cub" (quoted in Hummel, 1991).

A big male chasing a female over territorial rights in Alaska. (Karl Sommerer)

This orphaned cub in Alaska is searching for food on the tidal flats away from older bears. (Karl Sommerer)

Adolph Murie wrote of a grizzly *ménage-à-trois* in which a young grizzly, a large older male, and a female all traveled together, mated together, and slept "only a few feet apart" over a period of about three weeks (Murie, 1961).

There are also examples of apparent altruistic behavior in the world of the grizzly. In 1988, after a large male attacked a small Mc-

A friendly argument among subadult grizzlies. (Robert H. Busch)

Two grizzlies sparring in Alaska; note the cut nose on one bear. (Karl Sommerer)

Neil River cub that was separated from its mother, a second female temporarily adopted the injured cub and even nursed it. A few days later, it was adopted by yet another female, who left the game sanctuary with it two weeks later—a startling bit of behavior on the part of a supposedly vicious and cold-blooded animal.

Author Timothy Treadwell once observed in Alaska an injured male grizzly whose ribs showed through his fur and who had to drag his hind legs, which were either severely injured or broken. When a large female grizzly caught sight of the injured bear, she "walked directly up to him, and delicately kissed and caressed his face, lavishing him with love and attention" (Treadwell, 1997). Treadwell called the incident "the most beautiful few minutes of my life."

INTELLIGENCE

At one time, most philosophers agreed with French philosopher René Descartes that animals were not endowed with intelligence, only with instinct. In a letter to the Marquis of Newcastle, Descartes once wrote, "when swallows come in spring, they act in that like clocks," meaning that no thought went into their travels, only blind instinct.

Grizzlies are generally deemed to be quite intelligent, with large brains and the ability to learn from a single experience. (Robert H. Busch)

However, as early as 1739, there were a few dissenting voices regarding the intelligence of animals. In that year, philosopher David Hume stated that "no truth appe[a]rs to me more evident, than that beasts are endow'd with thought and reason as well as men." Over the past 200 years, biologists and philosophers alike have argued about whether Hume was right.

The main problem is that many human egos will not allow the belief that "lowly" creatures such as animals have the capacity to think, reason, or solve problems. In the minds of many strait-laced academics, admitting such beliefs would somehow threaten our own "superiority."

However, all except the very lowest of species demonstrate behavior that could be deemed "intelligence," a term that is difficult to define in animal terms. No single intelligence test has yet been developed that can be applied to a broad spectrum of species.

However, it is known that intelligence is linked with nervous system development. Progressively more complex organisms possess more elaborate differentiation of the nervous system, with increased development of the brain. It is in the mammals that the most complex nervous systems are seen.

Encephalization—the degree of head development relative to the rest of the body—has also reached its peak with the development of mammals.

The trend toward increased brain size began about 400 million years ago. Many mammal species showed an increased brain size over time, but then around 40 million years ago, their brain development stopped, and their brains today are very similar to those of their ancestors 40 million years ago. Moles, shrews, and hedgehogs all belong to this group. It is not known what stopped their rate of brain growth.

The brains of carnivores, however, continued to show an increase in brain size, and the brains of today's carnivores are larger than those of their ancestors. And among the carnivores, grizzlies have the largest brain relative to body size of any terrestrial carnivore.

In grizzlies and other higher mammals, the outer layer of the brain, the cerebral cortex, is very large compared to the total brain volume. The cortex covers the cerebrum, the largest and most complex portion of the brain. It has crucial sensory, motor, and associative functions and thus is partly responsible for what humans call intelligence.

In grizzlies, about 45 percent of the brain is cortex. In comparison, the cortex of a mouse is only about 30 percent of total brain volume; the cortex of a chimpanzee is about 55 percent of total brain volume.

Grizzlies are generally regarded as very intelligent, capable of learning from a single experience and capable of solving simple problems.

The bear sitting down in this photo seems to be having a good belly-laugh. It is hard not to anthropomorphize a creature so similar to humans. (Robert H. Busch)

Doug Seus, an animal trainer from Utah who has trained dozens of animals for television and feature films, is the owner of Bart, a 1,500-pound (682-kg) Kodiak bear. Seus says, "I train black bears, wolves, and cougars for film work too. My grizzlies and Kodiaks are the hardest to tame, but the easiest to train; generally, you only have to teach them something once" (quoted in Chadwick, 1986).

Behaviorists studying animal intelligence use a number of criteria to evaluate their subjects, including the ability of the animal to learn, especially from a single experience; the ability to form concepts; and the ability to combine experiences into a single pattern, a process which humans call reasoning. The ability to benefit or learn from the experiences of others is another factor in intelligence.

Conscious thinking and self-awareness are often associated with intelligence. Lance A. Olsen of the University of Montana believes that the ability of grizzlies to find hiding spots where they can see but not be seen demonstrates a degree of conscious thinking that goes beyond pure instinct.

Because of a lack of a direct system of measuring animal intelligence, most information available on the subject is anecdotal. How-

Even when you're a majestic grizzly, sometimes you just have to scratch. (Robert McCaw)

ever, as behaviorist D. C. Dennett points out, "ethologists know how misleading and, officially, unusable anecdotes are, and yet on the other hand they are often so telling" (quoted in Mortenson, 1987).

Anecdotes abound of bears using rocks to spring traps, for example, a clear demonstration of a bear's ability to learn and adapt to a situation.

Author Timothy Treadwell, who spent many years watching grizzlies in southern Alaska, tells an interesting anecdote about a family of grizzlies trying to ascend a steep ridge. The big mother bear had no problem, but her cubs were struggling. The mother bear then "dug holes in the earth, which served as a ladder for her tiny spring cubs. One by one, the miniature bears ascended the homemade steps, then disappeared" (Treadwell, 1997).

British Columbia grizzly biologist Bruce McLellan tells an interesting anecdote on grizzly intelligence that involves a female grizzly that was originally darted in the rear and then set free. Much later, she was caught in a foot snare. When the biologist approached, "she had dug a hole in the ground and was sitting in it in order to protect her butt from being hit by the tranquilizing dart. She had remembered the previous capture three years ago" (quoted in Domico, 1988).

As Alberta bear biologist Rob Wielgus jokingly says, the average grizzly bear is "always smarter than your average grizzly bear researcher" (quoted in Hummel, 1991).

GRIZZLY-BLACK BEAR RELATIONSHIPS

Compared to the mighty grizzly, the black bear is lighter, weaker, and usually less aggressive. Black bears have smaller home ranges and a greater adaptability to human activities, often learning to adapt to human ways when the grizzly chooses to move elsewhere.

Because black bears tend to feed more often during the day, and grizzlies tend to be crepuscular, encounters between the two species are kept to a minimum. When meetings do occur, the black bear is usually submissive, fleeing whenever possible. There are many instances of grizzlies attacking and killing black bears, especially cubs, and one documented account from 1997 of a grizzly digging out a hibernating black bear and eating it.

The black bear often takes over ranges vacated by the grizzly, such as this logged-over area in central Alberta. (Robert H. Busch)

In competition for food, the larger grizzly usually displaces the black bear. But when grizzly populations decline, the black bear is quick to take over. As grizzlies declined west of Canada's Hudson Bay, black bears took over the former grizzly territory. A similar situation occured in central Alberta's Swan Hills area, when black bears extended their range into the hills as grizzlies declined. Similar interrelationships have been noted between wolves and coyotes, with the latter spreading rapidly as wolf populations across the continent have plunged. Mother Nature, it seems, abhors a vacuum.

CHAPTER

4

Of Bears and Men

They're an extremely adaptable animal, . . . but they're not adaptable to being shot.

BRUCE MCLELLAN, 1991

At one time, the grizzly roamed over much of North America. Although its range did not reach the East Coast, its limits extended as far as Minnesota, Kansas, and Nebraska (see map in Chapter 1). In Canada, the great bear once roamed as far east as central Manitoba.

The grizzly used to be abundant across much of the continent. In 1824, explorer James Ohio Pattie claimed to have encountered more than 200 grizzlies in one day's travel in the mountains of Colorado. Ernest Thompson Seton wrote that in the Black Hills of South Dakota, great numbers of grizzlies traveled "in bands like buffalo," and were treated with great respect by the local natives.

GRIZZLIES AND NATIVE AMERICANS

It is not surprising that early natives both feared and revered the great grizzly. Some saw a grizzly kill as a badge of courage; historian George Bird Grinnell wrote, "the death of a bear gives the warrior greater re-known than the scalp of a human enemy." Others held the bear in such awe that it was taboo to even mention its name. The Blackfeet called it "The Unmentionable One" or "The Real Bear" (*nitakyaio*). They called the black bear merely "Bear" (*kyaio*), denoting its lesser status.

Explorers Meriwether Lewis and John Clark wrote an entry in their expedition journal for April 29, 1805, reporting that "Indians who go in quest of him [the grizzly] paint themselves and perform all the superstitious rites customary when they make war on a neighbor-ing nation."

Of course, sometimes the grizzly did not appreciate the reverence shown it by the local natives. Claude Jean Allouez, a European mis-sionary to the Pacific Northwest, wrote in 1666 about a tribe of Na-tive Americans who "live on raw fish; but these people, in turn, are eaten by bears of frightful size . . . with prodigiously long claws."

Anthropologist Richard Nelson wrote in his classic book, *Make Prayers to the Raven,* that among Alaska's Koyukon Indians, even the hide of a grizzly was a spiritual item: "It takes a few years for all that life to be gone from a brown bear's hide. That's the kind of power it has."

The Koyukon, after killing a bear, remove its feet, to prevent its spirit from wandering. Grizzly meat is not brought into a Koyukon vil-lage immediately after the kill, for "it is too fresh and potent, with

The White Cloud, Head Chief of the Iowas by George Catlin (1844/45). (National Gallery of Art, Paul Mellon Collection, Washington DC). Note the necklace of grizzly claws.

easily affronted spiritual energy." Women are not allowed to touch the meat or hide, echoing a belief among Native Americans that the grizzly bear spirit is too powerful for women to handle.

In many tribes, a necklace of grizzly claws was thought to bestow great courage and strength on the wearer. Many early artists painted Native Americans proudly wearing their necklaces of grizzly claws. In 1862, Frederick Verner painted an oil rendition of *Ne-bah-quah-om* (Big Dog), a Chippewa native wearing a claw necklace. In 1833–34,

Grizzly bear feast dish, by native carver Henry Hunt. (Royal British Columbia Museum, CPN 13854)

Karl Bodmer did a similar portrait of *Mahchsi Karehde,* a Mandan Indian. Most famous of all is likely George Catlin's *The White Cloud, Chief of the Tribe* (1844), which portrays an Iowa chief bedecked in bear claws.

Grizzly claws were thought to be steeped in power. Shamans of the Tlingit tribe of southeastern Alaska touched grizzly claws to a sick patient to induce healing. The sound of the claws rattled together was supposed to summon the powerful healing spirits of the grizzly.

Blackfoot Indian expert John C. Ewers, in his 1958 book *The Black-feet, Raiders on the Northwest Plains,* described the power of grizzly claws to young Blackfeet: "Adventurous young men hunted the powerful grizzly bear for its claws, which they proudly displayed in the form of necklaces. However, most Blackfoot Indians feared and avoided this dangerous beast. They regarded it as a sacred animal of great supernatural as well as physical power." To the Blackfoot, the grizzly was part bear and part human. Only the buffalo received greater veneration.

The Kwakiutl natives of the British Columbia coast believed that after killing a grizzly, the hunter absorbed the bear's fishing ability, strength, and ferocity. A killed bear was often treated as an honored guest, and was set in an upright sitting position, with food set before it.

A Haida carving of a
Bear Mother figure.
(Royal British Columbia
Museum, CPN 248 v.2)

The Shasta natives of California believed that if a man sat down
quietly and did not flee from a grizzly, it would sit down and speak
with him.

British Columbia's Haida natives told their children the legend
of the Bear Mother, in which a woman marries a grizzly and their
children become the ancestors of all Indians, giving them strength
and the ability to survive in the wild. Many other Native American
tribes had similar legends, in which the grizzly was a nurturer or
mother figure.

There is even a contemporary legend, told in the Sierra Madre Occidental Mountains of Mexico of Juan Oso, about a half-man, half-bear who is the offspring of a female human and a male bear.

This legend is very similar to the "Bear Son" stories told by West Coast Native Americans, in which the offspring of a human mother and a male bear undergoes a series of heroic adventures while trying to establish his true identity.

Tlingit Native Bear Song

Whu! Bear!
Whu Whu!
So you say
Whu Whu Whu
You come
You're a fine young man
You grizzly bear
You crawl out of your fur
You come
I say *Whu Whu Whu!*
I throw grease in the fire
For you
Grizzly bear—
We're one.

Lilloet Native Bear Song

You were the first to die, greatest of beasts.
We respect you and shall treat you accordingly;
No woman will eat your flesh,
No dog insult you.
May the lesser animals all follow you
And die by our traps and arrows.
May we now kill plenty of game.

May the goods of those we gamble with
Follow us as we leave the play,
And come into our possession.
May the goods of those we play *lehol* with
Become completely ours,
Even as a beast that we have slain.

The Tlingits and Tsimshians, neighbors to the Haida, used to tell the story of a member of the Te'kwedi clan, who married a female grizzly and sired children that were borne and raised by her. When he returned to his human wife, his bear wife became angry and ordered him to bring food only to her children. He disobeyed, and was promptly killed. Forever after, the symbol of the Te'kwedi clan has been a grizzly.

In a legend told by the Utes, who used to inhabit what is now Colorado and Utah, the Ute natives believed that they were descended from the great bear and that it possessed great magical powers and wisdom. Their four-day-long Bear Dance strengthened the bond between the Utes and the bear, and was intended to rouse the bears from hibernation.

In Wyoming, a prominent landmark is Devil's Tower, an 865-foot (264-m) high mass of columnar basalt of volcanic origin. But to various native tribes, the tower was made by a grizzly long, long ago. The Kiowas, Cheyenne, and Sioux all believed that the long, grooved columns that make up the tower were the result of grizzly bear scratches on rocks, that then grew and stretched to the present height. The Kiowa and Sioux both called the tower *Mateo Tipi*, meaning "Grizzly Bear's Lodge."

California's Pomo Indians believed that good men went to Heaven after death, but that bad men stayed on Earth, in the shape of a grizzly. The Yosemite Indians named themselves after the great bear, for in their dialect, the word "Yosemite" meant grizzly.

The Pomos, neighbors of the Yosemites, had an initiation ceremony in which the young men of the tribe were welcomed into manhood. As part of this rite of passage, a male member of the tribe dressed as a female grizzly, holding raccoon skins that represented bear cubs. The man then raced back and forth in front of a dance-house, in which the young men were hiding. One by one, the initiates were pushed out into the path of the "grizzly," who knocked the youths down. When they were allowed back up, the young men imitated bears themselves, and after more ceremony and dancing, were declared to be men.

Native Americans in the Stikine region of northern British Columbia told the legend of a great flood crossing the land. According to the legend, the people who jumped into the water became seals and those who ran into the forests became grizzlies.

British Columbia's Thompson Indians painted their faces black as a token of respect when they killed an enemy warrior or a grizzly.

The Navajo of the American Southwest believed that grizzlies had supernatural powers and would not hurt a grizzly unless one had hurt a Navajo. In that case, the local medicine man sang of the bear's positive traits and apologized to its spirits for the coming retribution. To kill a grizzly for no reason, they believed, would lead to insanity.

Neither Shoshones nor Arapahoes would kill a grizzly nor tan its hide. The Shuswap Indians of central British Columbia were told by their elders not to kill grizzlies, because after the bears had been skinned, they looked just like humans.

Many other Native Americans identified just as closely with grizzlies: The Sauk Indians called the grizzly "Old Man," the Cree called him "Chief's Son," the Navajo called the grizzly "Fine Young Chief," and the Menominee called him "Elder Brother." Some tribes refused to eat grizzly flesh, for to do so would be tantamount to cannibalism.

When explorer Henry Kelsey crossed the Canadian plains in 1690 and killed a grizzly, his Native American companions were horrified. "It was a god," they said.

Many modern-day Native Americans still revere the great bear. In 1982, northern Montana natives held a "bear honoring" that was attended by Native Americans, biologists, New-Age counterculturists, and many other people who were simply curious.

The groups gathered in a meadow along the north fork of the Flathead River, just south of the Canadian border. Sacred fires, sweat lodges, chants, and dances all served to honor the greatest predator on the continent. And although outsiders may scoff, those who were there say some unusual things happened at the gathering.

One morning a bluebird appeared, much earlier than normal in the area, and perched at the side of a Native American Bird Medicine Woman. When one ceremony called for snow, 2 inches (5 cm) obligingly fell the night before. When a full moon was required, the clouds drifted away to reveal one. After three days of celebration, the grizzly and the gods who looked over it had earned a new respect from those who had gathered in that mystical meadow.

GRIZZLIES AND WHITE SETTLERS

One of the most shameful episodes in the story of relationships between animals and humans is the fate of the grizzly at the hands of white settlers in North America.

For example, the grizzly used to be abundant on the Canadian prairies. In 1666, French missionary Claude Jean Allouez observed grizzlies in what is now northern Manitoba. Allouez likely was the first white person in Canada to glimpse the great bear.

English explorer Henry Kelsey left York Factory on the shores of Hudson Bay in 1690 and spent the next two years exploring the Canadian plains. He wrote in his journal for August 2, 1691, of sighting "a great sort of a Bear which is Bigger than any White Bear and is neither White nor Black but silver hair'd."

English explorer and fur trader David Thompson recorded seeing numerous grizzlies near Alberta's Bow River in 1787, and "grizzled bears, but not too many," near the Red Deer River. Another British explorer, Alexander Mackenzie, reported grizzlies along the Peace River in northern Alberta in 1795.

By 1810, the small Alberta trading post at Rocky Mountain House had 33 grizzly hides in storage, which represented an indirect measure of the abundance of grizzlies in the region. In 1859, the Palliser expedition observed seven grizzlies along the South Saskatchewan River.

Hudson Bay Company fur trading records for 1871 to 1872 show that 750 grizzly pelts were taken by hunters and trappers in just a few months in what is now southwest Saskatchewan. As a result of such carnage, by the 1890s, grizzlies were rare east of the Rocky Mountains in Alberta.

"Roping a Wild Grizzly" by James Walker (1877). (Thomas Gilcrease Institute of American History and Art, Tulsa, OK)

In the United States, the decimation of the grizzly was even more rapid. Within a hundred years of their first contact with white settlers, 90 percent of the grizzlies in the lower 48 states had been destroyed.

Grizzlies were first encountered in the United States by Spanish settlers in California, where the lush coastal forests once held at least 10,000 grizzlies.

One of the first explorers to see the California grizzlies was likely Friar Antonio de la Ascension, who traveled with the Sebastian Vizcaino expedition to the Monterey area in 1602, and wrote of seeing grizzlies on the beaches. In 1769, the death of the first California grizzly killed by a white man was recorded. Subsequent conflicts between grizzlies and explorers or settlers sparked the devastation of the West Coast grizzly population, an eradication that has seldom been equalled in the sad annals of wildlife in North America.

In 1808, grizzlies were still such a novelty that American soldier and explorer Zebulon Pike (for whom Colorado's Pikes Peak is named) gave two live grizzly cubs to President Thomas Jefferson to show just how different they were from the more familiar eastern black bear. There may have been 50,000 to 100,000 grizzlies in the lower 48 states at that time.

Early Californian settlers killed the grizzlies by roping them with strong lariats called *reatas*. A roped grizzly was usually stabbed to death, but sometimes two riders roped opposite ends of a bear and literally pulled it apart. Even the Spanish priests joined in these cruel

"Roping a Grizzly," by Charles Russell (1903). (Buffalo Bill Historical Center, Cody, WY)

hunts; one account tells of a Father Réal, who "was often known to go with young men on moonlight rides, lassoing grizzly bears."

Early settlers in California often reported seeing 50 grizzlies in one day. In 1827, a California writer with the memorable name of Duhaut Cilly claimed that grizzlies were so common around San Francisco that "they are often seen in herds." In 1831, George Yount, an early settler in the Napa Valley of California, stated that grizzlies "were everywhere upon the plains, in the valleys, and on the mountains . . . it was not unusual to see 50 to 60 within the 24 hours." One 1852 report stated that "schools [were] closed because [it was] unsafe for children to use trails." Old Ephraim, as the grizzly was called, was everywhere.

Grizzly steaks became a common food item and bear grease was used to lubricate the wooden wheels of carts. One enterprising California hunter named Oliver Allen made history when he used a whaling gun to kill the big bears.

FAMOUS "OUTLAW" GRIZZLIES

Old Ephraim   Old Ephraim was named after Ephraim, a Biblical character who was the leader of a warlike tribe. Famed as a cattle killer, Old Ephraim was chased for over a dozen years, beginning in 1911.

The "rogue" grizzly was finally trapped in northern Utah on August 22, 1923, in a 27-pound (12-kg) bear trap set in a pool where the bear liked to wallow. Old Ephraim was then shot by range conservationist Frank Clark. Clark had chased the bear from 1914 until he finally caught up with the bear nine years later.

Upon his death, Old Ephraim was found to have one deformed toe and to weigh 1,100 pounds (500 kg). His body was buried near Clark's campsite in Cache County, Utah.

Originally, a wooden marker marked the spot of Old Ephraim's grave. In 1966, the Boy Scouts of America replaced the old marker with a 9-foot- (3-m-) high memorial of natural stone. The plaque on the grave reads:

Old Ephraim's Grave (Grizzly Bear)
Killed by Frank Clark, Malad, Idaho
August 22, 1923—weight approx.
1100 pounds—height 9 ft. 11 in.
Smithsonian Institute has Ephraim's skull

El Casador   El Casador (Spanish for "The Hunter") allegedly killed numerous cattle and sheep in California in the 1800s. A hunter shot part of the bear's paw off, which gave the bear a distinctive track. El Casador was finally shot by Juan Francisco Dana, whose grandfather was provisional governor of Mexican California.

Old Mose   Old Mose was a Colorado bear who reputedly killed 800 head of cattle and five men before finally being shot near Canon City in southern Colorado in 1904, after 35 years of pursuit (making the bear almost impossibly old). The bear was found to weigh 900 pounds (409 kg) and his pelt was 10 feet (3 m) long.

Susie   Susie was a large bear famed as a cattle killer in the American Southwest. She was chased for three years by various ranchers, but was finally shot in 1883 by rancher Montague Stevens in the Crosby Mountains of New Mexico. He described his hunt in *Meet Mr. Grizzly* (1943).

Big Foot Wallace   Big Foot Wallace was a large silvertip who prowled the Platte River valley in Wyoming. His track was characterized by the fact that two toes of his left front paw were missing. Big Foot was shot in 1885 by Bryant B. Brooks, owner of the famed V-V Ranch.

Three Toes   Three Toes, who lost two toes to a leg-hold trap, killed a man in an early skirmish, and was thereafter also known as Man Killer. Three Toes was shot in Wyoming's Bighorn Mountains, sometime between 1912 and 1915.

Wab   Ernest Thompson Seton's famous fictional book, *The Biography of a Grizzly* (1900), was based on an actual bear known as Wab or Wahb. Wab was a big male grizzly condemned for killing cows in the Piney Creek area of Wyoming. Wab was finally shot in the 1890s by rancher A. A. Anderson, owner of the Palette Ranch.

Old Bigfoot   Old Bigfoot was made famous by Aldo Leopold's essay "Escudilla," included in his classic book, *A Sand Country Almanac* (1949). Old Bigfoot was killed on Escudilla Mountain in Apache County, Arizona, in June 1910. His skull is in the National Museum in Washington, D.C.

Old Silverback   Little is known about Old Silverback, other than the fact that he was a 1,000-pound (305-kg) male grizzly that terrorized Lamar Valley in the early days of Yellowstone National Park.

The great bears soon came into conflict with humans, who attempted with little effect to protect their livestock from the huge predators. Major Horace Bell, an early California newspaperman, recounted in his 1881 book, *Reminiscences of a Ranger,* that "in the [18]50s the grizzly bears were more plentiful in Southern California than pigs . . . [they were] so numerous in certain localities . . . as to make the rearing of cattle utterly impossible."

Impossible, that is, until 1848, when Sharps marketed the first breech-loaded rifle, replacing the clumsy old muzzle-loaders. This simple development, unheralded at first, spelled doom for the coastal grizzlies. As Montana nature writer Gary Turbak (1993) once wrote, "Grizzlies had claws and jaws, but the people had weapons."

As humans gained mastery over the big bear through sheer firepower, fear gave rise to incredibly cruel "sports" reminiscent of gladiator combat in the bad old days of the Roman coliseum.

For example, bear-baiting was common sport during California's roaring gold-rush days. Major Horace Bell recalled in his 1930 book, *On the Old West Coast,* that "In the great fiestas of time past at the Missions and Presidios there was always a bull and bear fight for the entertainment of the crowd. The last one on record that I know of took place at Pala . . . at the once-great Mission in San Luis Rey, in the mountains of San Diego County nearly 50 years ago."

In these inane duels, the front hoof of a bull was roped to the rear paw of a bear. The two were then released in a pen to fight to the death, while the crowd watched and wagered. This gory entertainment lasted well into the end of the 1800s.

In a sad variation on the theme, in the 1920s, one of the last California grizzlies was sent to Monterrey, Mexico, where it was set against an African lion. It was reported that the bear "killed him so quickly that the big audience hardly knew how it was done." The fate of the victorious bear was not mentioned.

Early Californians also trapped the big bear in box traps. An open box was placed in grizzly country with bait inside and a loop of rope was placed just inside the entrance to snare the bear's foot. When the rope was pulled by a struggling bear, the trap door fell shut. The bear was then dispatched with spears.

But it was primarily the Sharps rifle that allowed an unprecedented degree of slaughter. In Oregon, five hunters emerged after a year of hunting in 1848 with a grand total of 700 grizzly pelts. Within 40 years of the first influx of settlers to Oregon in 1852, the state's

"S. E. HOLLISTER, THE GREAT AMERICAN HUNTER & TRAPPER."
His famous encounter with the enormous, SHE BEAR while capturing her CUBS, in the Sierra Nevada Mountains, between the American and Mocosume rivers, California, in March, 1853.

A hand-colored lithograph, circa 1863, by Henry C. Eno, entitled "S. E. Hollister, The Great American Hunter and Trapper." (Amon Carter Museum, Forth Worth, TX)

grizzly's population had been completely wiped out. By 1890, the last American Plains grizzly was gone.

A number of early California hunters claimed to have each killed over 200 grizzlies within a single year. Within a hundred years of the invention of the Sharps rifle, the California grizzly had been hunted to extinction. The "golden bear," the very symbol of the state, was gone forever.

The rapid devastation of the California grizzly population was paralleled across the country. Whenever an explorer or settler met a bear, the animal usually paid for the meeting with its life. When Lewis and Clark trekked to the Missouri River in 1805, they spotted a grizzly and "immediately went to attack him," callously noting: "it is astonishing to see the wounds [these animals] will bear before they can be put to death." Lewis and Clark described the grizzly as "a furious and formidable animal." In their expedition from St. Louis to the West Coast, the explorers and their party managed to shoot more than 43 grizzlies.

Conflicts between humans and grizzlies led to some notable confrontations. In 1823, a man named Hugh Glass was mauled by a grizzly in what is now South Dakota. Left to die by his companions, Glass stumbled and crawled 100 miles (151 km) to Fort Kiowa, Montana, where he recuperated and lived to tell his tale.

FAMOUS EARLY GRIZZLY HUNTERS

James Bridger was a hunter and guide in the Rocky Mountains of the western United States in the mid-1800s.

Don Jose Ramón Carrillo was an aristocrat in California in the late 1800s. He was famous for fighting grizzlies with a light sword.

Allen Hasselborg killed many bears on Alaska's Admiralty Island in the early 1900s and was once seriously mauled by one of his intended victims.

"Bear" Howard was a hunter and rancher in Arizona in the 1800s. He was one of the first to sell American grizzly gall bladders to Chinese merchants.

"Old Ike" killed over a hundred bears in the late 1800s. In 1886, he wounded a grizzly near the headwaters of the Salmon River in Idaho. The bear turned and charged, crushing Ike's chest and killing him.

James A. "Bear" Moore was badly mauled by a grizzly in 1883. He sought vengeance thereafter, killing many bears, including one that he killed using only a knife.

George Nidever was a grizzly hunter in the early days of San Luis Obispo County in California. By some counts, Nidever killed 45 grizzlies in the year 1837 alone, and almost 200 in his whole career.

Ramon Ortega hunted in Ventura County, California, in the late 1800s. He also was reported to have killed 200 bears in his career, including 15 in one day.

William Pickett hunted grizzlies in the early days of Yellowstone National Park, and is rumored to have killed more than 70 grizzlies in that area.

Theodore Roosevelt was not only a President, but also a keen hunter, rancher, soldier, conservationist, and writer. He pursued the grizzly, which he considered his favorite big game animal, throughout many states, although the total number he killed is not known.

Andy Sublette pursued the grizzly across the United States in the mid-1800s. He kept two grizzly cubs as pets, and was badly mauled by a grizzly in 1853. While hunting grizzlies in 1854 in

California, Sublette wounded a bear which turned and attacked. He died of his injuries a few days later.

James St. Clair Willburn hunted grizzlies throughout Trinity County, California, in the mid-1800s.

William Wright was a hunter who was rumored to have once killed five grizzlies with five shots in five minutes. He published *The Grizzly Bear: The Narrative of a Hunter-Naturalist* in 1909, complete with some of the earliest black and white photos of the great bear.

George Yount was one of the first settlers in the Napa Valley of California. Yount claimed to have often killed five grizzlies in one day, and requested that a bear be carved on his gravestone.

By the late 1800s, grizzlies were becoming rare in most areas. Author Enos Mills wrote in his 1919 book, *The Grizzly, Our Greatest Wild Animal,* "When I arrived in Colorado in 1884, grizzlies were still common throughout the mountain areas of the state." Just a few years later, the grizzly apparently was in a rapid decline.

"Uncle" Dick Wootton, a pioneer frontiersman in the Rocky Mountains, stated in 1890 that "There used to be a great many of them in the mountains but we rarely hear of one now." Theodore Roosevelt echoed this sentiment in his 1893 book, *The Works of Theodore Roosevelt,* with the comment that "The grisly is now chiefly a beast of the high hills and heavy timber . . . he has learned that he must rely on cover to guard him from man."

By the 1880s and 1890s, many jurisdictions had placed bounties on the grizzly. One of the earliest was passed in 1793, when the parliament of Upper Canada passed "An Act to Encourage the Destruction of Wolves and Bears."

By 1904, a grizzly pelt was worth $75, over a month's wages at the time.

That same year, naturalist William Hornaday wrote in his book *The American Natural History* that the grizzly's "name and fame inspired terror throughout the mountains and foothills of the wild western domain which constituted its home."

In 1915, the U.S. government established the Animal Damage Control Program, which gave bounty hunters and animal control agents sweeping powers for "the destruction of mountain lions, wolves, coyotes, . . . and other animals [deemed] injurious to agriculture, horticulture, forestry, husbandry, game, or domestic animals."

GRIZZLY ADAMS

One of the most colorful characters associated with grizzlies was John (sometimes listed as James) Capen "Grizzly" Adams.

Adams was born in 1912 in Massachusetts, where he worked at a variety of odd jobs, including shoemaker, trapper, and circus hand.

"Grizzly" Adams, from an 1860 engraving in *The Adventures of James Capen Adams, Mountaineer and Grizzly Bear Hunter of California* by Theodore Hittell.

In 1849, the California gold rush lured Adams west. While exploring the rugged western wilderness, Adams captured two young grizzly cubs, whom he later named Lady Washington and Ben Franklin. The two unfortunate cubs were beaten into submission and became the most famous of the "trained" grizzlies that were to give Adams his nickname.

Adams ended up in San Francisco, where he walked the bears on lengths of chain through the streets. He also established a Mountaineer's Museum, where he kept a small menagerie of cougars, deer, and other animals.

Despite his fame as a self-taught naturalist, Adams was more of a hunter than a conservationist. Naturalist A. Starker Leopold once claimed that Adams was one of those most responsible for the extirpation of the grizzly bear in California.

Adams' fame spread with the 1860 publication of a book entitled *The Adventures of James Capen Adams, Mountaineer and Grizzly Bear Hunter of California,* by Theodore Hittell.

A hundred years later, Adams' fame soared again, when a popular television series was named after him.

"Grizzly" Adams died in his home state of Massachusetts in 1860.

(The program still continues today, under the euphemistic title of Wildlife Services.) Bounty hunters and animal control agents alike began to track down the few remaining grizzlies, and state by state, the last grizzly died.

Some of the early bounty hunters became legendary figures. Probably the most famous of them all was Ben Lilly. Born Vernon Lilly in Alabama in 1856, Lilly moved to Mexico in 1908 and then to the southwestern United States in 1911. In that year, he killed three of the last grizzlies in New Mexico.

Lilly was hired by the Biological Survey (now called the U.S. Fish and Wildlife Service) in 1916 to help eradicate predatory animals and was paid the princely sum of $200 per month. Whenever a wolf, bear, or cougar was spotted, Lilly was the man called in to shoot the beast.

During his years as a bounty hunter and trapper, Lilly claimed to have killed over 400 bears, many of them grizzlies. He died in 1936, but his fame grew following the 1950 publication *The Ben Lilly Legend,* by J. Frank Dobie.

By 1920, a grizzly hide was worth $120, but in the lower 48 states, there were few grizzlies left for bounty hunters to chase.

Canada still was well stocked with grizzlies, though. In 1932, the *New York Sun* reported that Alberta guide James Brewster had personally shot 146 grizzlies in the Banff-Jasper area of the Canadian Rockies.

DOCUMENTED "LAST GRIZZLIES"

Arizona   Arizona's last grizzly was long thought to be a 2-year-old, 200-pound (91-kg) bear shot by hunter Richard R. Miller on September 13, 1935, in Greenlee County, Arizona. However, Arizona author David E. Brown has found an account stating that trapper B. B. Folk killed an immature grizzly on the northwest slope of Mount Baldy in the White Mountains on the Fort Apache Indian Reservation in the summer of 1939.

California   California's last "golden bear" was shot by rancher Jesse B. Agnew in August 1922, in Horse Corral Meadow, Tulare County.

Colorado   Long thought to be extirpated since the 1950s, Colorado's last grizzly was killed with an arrow by hunting guide Ed Wiseman on September 23, 1979, in the San Juan Mountains near the southern edge of the state.

Manitoba   Manitoba's last grizzly, one of the last plains grizzlies in Canada, was shot in 1923, near Duck Mountain in the southwest corner of the province.

Nevada   Nevada's last grizzly was probably one killed by Charles Foley in 1907 near Silver Creek, Nevada.

New Mexico   The last grizzly in New Mexico was allegedly shot by Tom Campbell in 1933 in the Jemez Mountains. However, there is a skull dated 1935 from Magdalena Baldy, western New Mexico, in the U.S. National Museum in Washington, D.C.

North Dakota   North Dakota's last grizzly was shot by Dave Warren in the fall of 1897 near Oakdale, along the eastern edge of the Killdeer Mountains.

Oregon   Government trapper Evan Stonemen killed Oregon's last grizzly on September 14, 1931, in Wallowa County.

Saskatchewan   Saskatchewan's last grizzly was allegedly killed in 1906 in the Cypress Hills in the southwest corner of the province. However, there are undocumented accounts of grizzlies that were still living in the Pasquia Hills of eastern Saskatchewan as late as the 1930s.

Texas   A joint effort by C. O. Finley, John Z. Means, and a pack of 52 dogs finally brought down Texas's last grizzly, an old 1,100-pound (500-kg) male, in October 1890.

Utah   Utah's last grizzly was the famous Old Ephraim (see box on "Famous Outlaw Grizzlies" on page 00). He was killed by Frank Clark on August 22, 1923, in Cache County in northern Utah.

The documented dates of "last grizzly" killings follow the spread of settlers across the West: Texas, 1890; North Dakota, 1897; California, 1922; Utah, 1923; Oregon and New Mexico, 1935; and Arizona, 1939. In Canada, the last grizzly in Manitoba was shot in 1923 in the Duck Mountains in the southwest corner of the province. Saskatchewan's last grizzlies hung on into the 1930s in the Pasquia Hills in the eastern part of the province.

In those early days of the West, no one worried about the future of the great bear. Pioneer conservationist Aldo Leopold wrote in *A Sand County Almanac:* "In 1909, when I first saw the West, there were grizzlies in every major mountain pass, but you could travel for months without meeting a conservation officer."

Conservation officers were badly needed, however, for settlers were quick to shoot first and ask questions later. From the late 1800s to the 1940s and 1950s, ranchers routinely shot grizzlies on sight to protect their stock, even when there was no evidence that predation had occurred. By the 1950s, the range of the grizzly in Canada had shrunk to about three-quarters of its original extent.

The big bears were slow to gain legal protection and were subject to changing attitudes on the part of game managers.

The case of Alberta is typical. Bears were not even mentioned in the Game Acts of the Statutes of Alberta between 1907 and 1927. An Order in Council in August 1927 finally gave grizzlies protection as big game animals, restricting the hunting of grizzlies to one bear per year, after purchase of a $5 permit. The Order prohibited the hunting of bears less than 1 year of age, or of females with cubs.

By the 1940s, wild bears had become "bad guys" in the eyes of many U.S. and Canadian wildlife managers. In the 1944 Annual Report from the province of Alberta, bears were officially labeled "a menace to livestock." All protection was withdrawn, and the only place where it was illegal to shoot a grizzly was within the limits of provincial forest reserves.

Even bears in forest reserves were not completely safe, however. The 1948 Annual Report recognized that the Alberta government had entered the ranks of active bear managers, stating that "the Department employs special hunters to kill any Grizzly Bear in the Forest Reserves and the Waterton-Carbondale Game Preserves." Many grizzlies were shot during this dark period of grizzly management and in the decade that followed.

SMOKEY THE BEAR

One of the most famous bears of all time was Smokey the Bear, a fictitious advertising character used to promote fire safety in the woods. Although it was never specified what species Smokey was, he was always portrayed as a brown bear, and is thought to have been modeled after a Yellowstone grizzly.

One of the strangest incidents in World War II came when a Japanese submarine shelled the southern California coast. Alarmed that future attacks might start huge fires along the American coast, forestry officials organized a forest-fire prevention program. Initially, wartime slogans were used to promote the program, but in 1944, the Disney cartoon character Bambi was added to a program poster, with great success. The Wartime Advertising

Poster of Smokey the Bear.

Council and the U.S. Forest Service decided to create a new campaign, this time featuring a bear.

The result was a character called Smokey the Bear, named after "Smokey" Joe Martin, assistant chief of the New York City Fire Department from 1919 to 1930. Artists drew a brown bear dressed in blue jeans and wearing a wide-brimmed ranger's hat, and armed the bear with a shovel. An advertising agent coined that now-famous phrase, "Remember, only *you* can prevent forest fires," and a star was born.

By the 1950s, the campaign was so well known that the U.S. Congress passed a Smokey Bear Act to protect the advertising character's image.

In 1950, a forest fire spread through the Lincoln National Forest in New Mexico, leaving behind a trail of destruction and a badly burned black bear cub found clinging to a tree. The little cub was rescued by firefighters and flown to Santa Fe for veterinary care. After the cub was nursed back to health, it was dubbed "Smokey," after the advertising character, and became the living mascot of the U.S. Forest Service.

Smokey was sent to the U.S. National Zoo in Washington, D.C., where he lived out the rest of his days in comfort. Smokey died on November 6, 1976.

During this same period, an early territorial governor of Alaska (quoted in Walker, 1993) contended angrily, "Alaska will never make progress until we eliminate brown and grizzly bears." In the 1950s, one Alaska governor ordered that grizzlies on Kodiak Island be strafed by a gun mounted on an aircraft as a "control" measure. Thirty-five dead bears were the result.

From the 1940s up until the mid-1980s, indiscriminate poisoning programs, aimed at ridding the wild of coyotes and other "varmints" deemed incompatible with livestock, killed dozens of innocent grizzlies across North America. As late as 1985, a grizzly died from a strychnine poisoning campaign in the Yukon.

It was not until the 1960s that humans suddenly awoke to the fact that many species of life on Earth were in peril. An Alberta Fish and Wildlife Division internal memorandum dated June 6, 1961, stated that "much misunderstanding has arisen regarding bear[s]."

The memo deplored the "indiscriminate trapping and killing of bear, particularly grizzly bear."

The province's first survey of hunter harvest of grizzlies did not take place until 1968. The fall hunting season for grizzlies was closed in 1970. Although grizzly populations slowly began to increase, hunting pressure was still intense. The 1990 *Management Plan for Grizzly Bears in Alberta* reviewed hunting statistics and concluded that "The provincial grizzly bear population has been overexploited in recent years."

The plan recommended a provincial population of 1,000 grizzlies. At that time, the Alberta grizzly population was about 790 bears. Ten years later, the population is about the same, and the goal of a thousand bears seems a long, long, way off.

The Grizzly as a Game Animal

In 1691, English explorer Henry Kelsey surprised a grizzly on a moose kill near Nelson River, in what is now northern Manitoba. He promptly shot the bear, which is believed to be the first of many western grizzlies to be killed by the white man in North America.

As early as 1887, an article by hunter George O. Shields in *Harper's New Monthly Magazine* stated that "grizzly bear hunting is unquestionably the greatest sport that our continent can afford." Many hunters traveled great distances to match wits and firepower with the greatest predator on the continent.

But by 1913, American conservationist William Hornaday would write in *Our Vanishing Wildlife,* "outside of our game preserves, I know of not one locality in which grizzly bears are sufficiently numerous to justify a sportsman in going out to hunt them." Hornaday called for closing the season on grizzlies in California, Montana, Wyoming, Washington, Idaho, and Oregon for five years, "to give our bears protection of some sort." It is a pity that no one listened to Hornaday's words, for within 25 years of his statement, the grizzly populations of California and Oregon were a matter of history.

Luckily for the grizzly, attitudes toward irresponsible hunting and over-hunting of threatened species have changed a great deal in the past century.

According to the 1996 U.S. Fish and Wildlife Service National Survey of Fishing, Hunting, and Wildlife-Associated Recreation, only about one in ten of American adults hunts. From 1980 to 1995, the

BART THE BEAR™

Perhaps the most famous of modern grizzlies was Bart, a 1,500-pound (682-kg) male Kodiak bear who starred in many commercials, television shows, and feature films.

Bart was born on January 10, 1977, to a pair of captive grizzly bears at a zoo. His grandparents came from the Kodiak and Chichagof Islands off the coast of Alaska. When he was 5 weeks old, Bart was sold to animal trainer Doug Seus, owner of the Wasatch Rocky Mountain Wildlife Ranch located near Heber City, Utah.

Seus and his wife Lynne bottle-fed the baby until he was 11 months old and weighed 300 pounds (136 kg). At that point, they built the bear his own house.

When Bart was 8 years old and weighed about 1,000 pounds (454 kg), he strolled by two of Seus's tame deer, who promptly died of shock at the sight.

By the age of ten, Bart was getting so big that Seus had to take the bear in the back of a pickup truck to the local carwash for a bath.

Bart grew to be 9.5 feet (2.9 m) tall and consumed about 60 pounds (27 kg) of food a day. His house opened onto a spacious pasture with large cottonwoods, a stream, and a swimming hole.

Bart's training consisted of love and affection, with no force,  drugs, or tranquilizers. When he performed an action correctly, he was given a reward. His favorite treats were apples, pear juice, and carrots. He also liked hamburgers and pineapple milk shakes. Bart died on May 18, 2000, from cancer, at the age of 23.

Bart the Bear strikes a pose for the camera. (Fernandez & Peck/Adventure Photo & Film)

"Grizzly at Bay" by
William Robinson Leigh
(1915). (Buffalo Bill
Historical Center, Cody,
WY)

number of hunters decreased by 8 percent. Over that same period, the number of home-based wildlife-observers increased 96 percent and the number of people who traveled to watch wildlife increased 63 percent. A 1996 Angus Reid poll in British Columbia revealed that 91 percent of those surveyed opposed trophy hunting, and 77 percent wanted it banned altogether.

Hunting has also come under heavy fire from conservationists. Biologists have long tried to quantify how many bears can be safely taken from a given population without that population slowly decreasing to extinction.

In 1991, the Committee on the Status of Endangered Wildlife in Canada recommended 4 percent as the maximum total harvest rate for any given Canadian grizzly population.

The Committee identified 12 Bear Zones where the great bear still existed in Canada. In almost half of the zones, studies of official

"A. O. Wheeler and T. G. Longstaff with three dead grizzly bears, T. G. Longstaff's Bugaboo Trip, 1910." Photo by Byron Harmon. (Whyte Museum of the Canadian Rockies, Banff, AB. Byron Harmon Photograph Collection)

statistics showed that the bear was being overhunted. Add to that the number of problem bears killed illegally and the number of poached bears, and the magnitude of the overkill swells to serious proportions.

For example, the British Columbia Wildlife Branch currently quotes 10,000 to 13,000 as the "official" provincial grizzly population. However, this number may well be high; a number of conservationists have suggested the actual population is closer to 7,000. Veteran bear biologist Wayne McCrory believes it may even be as low as 5,000 to 6,000.

Of British Columbia's 5,000 to 13,000 grizzlies, an average of 350 per year are legally shot in the province by resident and nonresident hunters. The number of legal kills has been generally declining since 1991, reaching an all-time low of 238 in 1993. On average, another 20 grizzlies are killed annually as nuisance bears.

The number of grizzlies killed illegally is a matter of much dispute. A 1991 study by biologist Vivian Banci found that nonhunting kills of grizzlies had been underestimated in every jurisdiction in Canada.

A 1989 internal B.C. Wildlife Branch memo leaked to the Western Canada Wilderness Committee revealed that the number of illegal and unreported kills of grizzlies was almost equal to the legal kill. In some areas, the illegal kill may even be greater.

Researchers Andrew Trites and Harvey Thommasen did a survey of grizzly deaths in the Bella Coola watershed between 1975 and 1988, and found that of 89 grizzlies killed, 57 were killed as nuisance bears or illegally killed. The official number of grizzlies killed in the area (according to B.C. Wildlife Branch statistics) was 32, less than half the actual total. Add to that the number of poached bears that are never discovered, and the total provincial grizzly harvest may actually be as high as 10 percent of the grizzly population—more than twice the recommended harvest rate.

In other jurisdictions, grizzly harvest rates of 8 to 15 percent may be sustainable. Allowable mortality is dependent on the area's grizzly reproductive rate, age of first reproduction, litter size, and interval between litters. Generally speaking, harvest rates for black bears are much higher than for grizzlies, because of the higher population overall and the younger age for mature females at first litters. Recommended rates for allowable human-caused grizzly mortality across North America range from 4 percent in British Columbia to 10.5 percent in the Yukon.

But not just the size of the overall kill each year is important. Crucial to the survival of a grizzly population is the number of female grizzlies that survive to reproduce. In British Columbia, wildlife managers try for a male:female ratio of 65:35. Generally, harvest rates must allow for protection of female grizzlies, and most jurisdictions have included this provision in their regulations. Because many females are shot in May, when they are actively wandering in search of food for their cubs, many jurisdictions have either closed spring hunts altogether, or shortened the spring season to close by mid-May.

There is some evidence that trophy hunting can have negative effects on grizzly populations. In a ten-year study by Alberta biologist Robert Wielgus, it was discovered that most trophy grizzlies are large males.

Hunters in early spring are more likely to kill male grizzlies, for it is the males who leave the dens first. The removal of these adult males was found to cause an increase in the number of cubs eaten by young male bears. These young male bears establish new harems by forcing the female grizzlies into heat again by killing their cubs. It was also found that in many cases, females moved their cubs into less choice, food-poor areas to avoid the threat of young male grizzlies, threatening the long-term viability of the whole grizzly population.

Many trophy grizzlies are big males. The killing of these large adult males may alter the population dynamics in any given grizzly ecosystem. (Robert H. Busch)

In one study on the Alaskan Peninsula, 60 percent of all grizzlies shot were males. The average age of the grizzlies was 5 years (Walker, 1993).

An opposite view is held by some biologists, who believe that grizzly hunting is good for grizzlies. "Hunting makes grizzlies fear humans, and fearful grizzlies stand a much better chance of surviving—both as individuals and as a species," says Ray Demarchi, a biologist formerly with the B.C. Fish and Wildlife Branch (quoted in Turbak, 1984).

An additional negative factor in grizzly management is the distressing number of grizzlies that are accidentally shot each year by hunters who mistook them for black bears. One of the worst such incidents occurred in 1983, when hunters in northern Montana accidentally killed 5 grizzlies in 10 days. In Wyoming, nine grizzlies were mistakenly identified as black bears and were shot between 1982 and 1984.

Each year, over a thousand grizzlies are killed by hunters. Furthermore, one Yukon study found that 1 grizzly in 4 shot by hunters was only wounded.

The Yukon Ministry of Renewable Resources is also concerned about the difficulty of determining the sex of a bear in the field. Its Hunting Regulations Summary offers some excellent tips for sexing wild grizzlies at a distance, such as the fact that female grizzlies tend to urinate behind their back legs, whereas males urinate in front of their hind legs. The Yukon Hunting Regulations Summary also offers

A trophy grizzly shot near Telegraph Creek, British Columbia. (Edna Whalley Collection)

the questionable generality that grizzlies found in high alpine areas tend to be females. No other jurisdiction in North America offers such tips to their hunters.

Hunters must be taught how to properly dispose of gut piles left after a legal ungulate (elk or caribou) kill. Many hunters call the hunting of bears that come to feed on gut piles "legal baiting," and believe it is an easy way around the law. But it is a dangerous one: Two hunters near Radium, British Columbia, died in 1995 when a grizzly attracted to a gut pile took not only the pile, but also the two hunters' lives. Because of the inherent danger in hunting grizzly bears found over gut piles, many jurisdictions favor spring seasons, when no such legal bait is available.

GRIZZLY HUNTING REGULATIONS

Today, the great bear is legally hunted in only five jurisdictions: Alaska, Alberta, British Columbia, the Northwest Territories, and the Yukon.

A legal hunt was permitted in most areas of Montana, excluding the Cabinet-Yaak areas, until 1991. In August of that year, the International Fund for Animals filed suit in federal court to halt the hunting of grizzlies in Montana, contending the hunt was illegal under the Endangered Species Act. Joining the Fund were the Swan View Coalition, a Montana-based environmental group, and Jasper Carlton, director of the Biodiversity Legal Foundation.

The lawsuit was filed after Montana's first-ever spring grizzly hunt, in which three grizzlies were killed, including a prime 21½-year-old male.

"The state of Montana and the federal government are pandering to trophy hunters rather than protecting a rare and remarkable threatened species," said Wayne Pacelle, the national director of the International Fund for Animals (quoted in the *Calgary Herald,* 1991). "It is much more vital to preserve living bears in the wild than to preserve bears heads on hunters' walls."

Bowing to massive pressure, the Montana Department of Fish, Wildlife and Parks finally closed the state to grizzly hunting in late 1991.

Regulations Summary

In British Columbia, the grizzly hunting license fee is $80 for a resident and $530 for a nonresident. The bag limit is 1 animal per year. There is no open season for grizzlies in British Columbia. The province uses a limited entry system, in which hunters apply for a limited number of licenses for a certain hunting management area. Hunters are asked not to shoot "any grizzly bear or black bear when observed in a family unit."

Grizzlies that are shot in British Columbia must be submitted to a regional or subregional compulsory government inspection center. Both the skull and the hide, bearing either a testicle or part of the penis (in the case of males) or a mammary gland (in the case of females), must be submitted for inspection.

In 1973, British Columbia imposed a ban on the commercial trade in certain bear parts. The regulations forbid the possession, trafficking, importing, and exporting of bear galls, including any part of the gall bladder, and of genitalia. It also bans trade in bear paws, although possession is still permitted for personal use and for ceremonial use by native peoples.

Alberta charges resident grizzly hunters a draw levy ($3.04), a Wildlife Identification number fee ($8.00), a Wildlife Certificate fee

($22.85) and a Big Game License fee ($48.59), for a total of $82.48. Nonresidents must be accompanied by a Designated Guide or a Class C Guide. Grizzlies are hunted by a Special License, which is obtained through a draw (lottery) process. The license allows hunting of a specific species only in specific areas during a specified season. The bag limit is 1 grizzly per year.

Grizzlies that are shot must be registered at an Alberta Environmental Protection office. As in British Columbia, hunters must submit both the skull and skin with evidence of the bear's sex still attached at the time of inspection; this includes the scrotum in the case of a male bear and a teat or portion of a mammary gland in the case of a female.

In the Yukon, resident grizzly hunters pay a hunting license fee of $10 plus a $25 fee for a big game seal, for a total fee of only $35. Nonresident Canadians pay a license fee of $75, a seal fee of $25, and must be accompanied by a registered Yukon guide or outfitter. Nonresident non-Canadians pay a license fee of $150, a seal fee of $25, and must be accompanied by a registered Yukon outfitter. If a nonresident kills a grizzly, an additional trophy fee of $500 for male grizzlies and $750 for females is charged.

The north slope of the Yukon is closed to grizzly hunting except for hunters with special permits. An annual harvest of 5 bears has been set for this area.

The grizzly open season in the Yukon is generally from April through June 21 in the spring and from August 1 or 15 through November 30 in the fall. The bag limit is generally 1 grizzly every three license years; a few areas are open to only 1 kill a year.

The Yukon Ministry of Renewable Resources requests that hunters "avoid hunting bears that are travelling together," to avoid killing females. All females with cubs and all cubs less than 3 years old are protected.

The skull and hide with baculum attached must be inspected by a Yukon Conservation Officer or wildlife technician not later than ten days after the season closure or upon request of a Conservation Officer. Hunters who do not retain these parts will have their bear considered a female (subject to a higher fee) for trophy fee purposes.

In the Northwest Territories, resident grizzly hunters must pay only $10 for a license/tag. Nonresident Canadians pay $20 and nonresident non-Canadians, $50. If a bear is killed and the hunter wishes to export the animal or any part thereof, a trophy fee of

$1,000 must be paid. All nonresidents must be accompanied by a licensed guide provided by an outfitter.

Open season for grizzlies in the Northwest Territories stretches from August 15 through October 31 in the fall and from April 15 through May 31 in the spring. Not all areas are open during each season. The bag limit is any number of adult bears not accompanied by a cub. The Northwest Territories Department of Resources, Wildlife, and Economic Development defines a cub as a young bear with a hide measuring less than 4½ feet (1.4 m) from the tip of the nose to the end of the tail when fresh, or less than about 5 feet (1.6 m) when stretched and dried.

Alaskan residents must obtain a hunting license ($25) and a tag ($25), for a total of $50. Nonresidents must pay for a hunting license ($85) and a tag ($500) for a total of $585. Nonresident non-Americans must buy a license ($85) and a tag ($650) for a total of $735. Nonresident grizzly hunters must be accompanied by a guide or outfitter.

The grizzly open hunting season in Alaska generally runs from August 10 through December 31 in the fall and from March 15 through June 15 in the spring. The bag limit is 1 grizzly every year (July 1 through June 30) or 1 every four years, depending on the area.

It is illegal in Alaska to take grizzly cubs less than 2 years old or sows that are accompanied by cubs. It is also against the law to kill grizzlies within ½ mile (0.7 km) of garbage dumps or landfills.

Grizzlies taken within most game management units in Alaska must have a metal or plastic seal affixed to the hide and skull by a sealing officer. Evidence of sex (penis sheath or vaginal orifice) must be attached to the hide when it is sealed.

Region	Number of grizzlies killed in 1998
Alaska	1033
Alberta	13
British Columbia	209
Northwest Territories	25
Yukon	62

Sources: Alaska Department of Fish and Game, Alberta Department of Environmental Protection, B.C. Wildlife Branch, Yukon Ministry of Renewable Resources, and Northwest Territories Department of Resources, Wildlife and Economic Development.

RECORD GRIZZLIES

Since its founding in 1887, the Boone and Crockett Club has been recognized as the official record keepers of the hunting fraternity. The club began the recording of trophy animals in 1932 and developed a copyrighted point system of scoring based on skull width and length in 1950. (According to Boone and Crockett Club regulations, measurements cannot be taken until at least 60 days after the animal was killed. All flesh, membranes, and cartilage must be completely removed. Skull measurements are taken without the lower jaw. Greatest length is not measured along the skull itself, but along an imaginary line running through the long axis of the skull. Greatest width is measured along an imaginary line perpendicular to this axis.) The club divides grizzlies into two categories: the great Kodiak bear and the grizzly.

BOONE AND CROCKETT CLUB RECORD GRIZZLIES

The Boone and Crockett Club divides its grizzly hunting records into two categories: Alaska brown bear (Kodiak) and grizzly. The following are the top five trophy bears in each category. All measurements are in inches.

Alaska Brown Bear:

Score =	Length of skull +	width of skull	Locality	Date Killed
$30^{12}/_{16}$	$17^{15}/_{16}$	$12^{13}/_{16}$	Kodiak Island	1952
$30^{11}/_{16}$	$18^{10}/_{16}$	$12^{1}/_{16}$	Kodiak Island	1961
$30^{9}/_{16}$	$18^{7}/_{16}$	$12^{2}/_{16}$	Kodiak Island	1938
$30^{9}/_{16}$	$18^{12}/_{16}$	$11^{12}/_{16}$	Bear R., AK	1908
$30^{6}/_{16}$	18	$12^{6}/_{16}$	Kodiak Island	1966

Grizzly Bear:

Score =	Length of skull +	width of skull	Locality	Date Killed
$27^{2}/_{16}$	$17^{2}/_{16}$	$9^{12}/_{16}$	Bella Coola, B.C.	1970
$27^{2}/_{16}$	$16^{14}/_{16}$	$10^{4}/_{16}$	Dean River, B.C.	1982
$27^{2}/_{16}$	$17^{3}/_{16}$	$9^{15}/_{16}$	Inglutalik R., AK	1991
$26^{14}/_{16}$	$16^{14}/_{16}$	10	Tetlanika R., AK	1989
$26^{14}/_{16}$	$16^{6}/_{16}$	$10^{8}/_{16}$	Anahim L., B.C.	1990

Reprinted courtesy of the Boone and Crockett Club, 250 Station Drive, Missoula, MT 59801, (406)542–1888.

The Boone and Crockett Club record Kodiak bear was taken in late May 1952, near Karluk Lake on Kodiak Island, and scored $30^{12}\!/_{16}$ by the Boone and Crockett system. In comparison, the record polar bear scored $29^{15}\!/_{16}$ and the trophy black bear only $23^{10}\!/_{16}$.

The record Kodiak bear was taken as part of a scientific expedition headed by Melville N. Lincoln and sponsored by a group affiliated with the Los Angeles County Museum. The actual shot that killed the bear was made by Roy R. Lindsley, who was ironically an employee of the U.S. Fish and Wildlife Service in Kodiak. The trophy skull is still in the collection of the Los Angeles County Museum.

The Boone and Crockett Club trophy grizzly record is a three-way tie. One of the record skulls was picked up in western British Columbia's Bella Coola valley by bear hunter James Shelton in 1970. Another was killed by Roger J. Pentecost in the nearby Dean River valley in 1982. It took three shots to kill this huge bear, whose skull is now in the collection of Lynn Allen. The most recent record grizzly was shot by Theodore Kurdziel, Jr., in 1991 near the Inglutalik River on the coast east of Nome, Alaska.

CHAPTER

5

Grizzly Attacks

I could just hear the bones go crunch,
crunch, crunch, crunch.

Attack victim Sonja Crowley, 1998

For me, one of the most awesome aspects of the grizzly's nature is its sheer power. As grizzly biologist Bruce McLellan (quoted in Turbak, 1984) says, "It's a challenge to study an animal that could kill you instantly if it wanted."

In the early 1800s, explorer Meriwether Lewis wrote in his expedition journals that he would "rather fight two Indians than one bear." However, even when provoked, the great bear usually shows a placid nature. Although explorer Henry Kelsey declared in 1691 that "He is man's food and he makes food of man," grizzly attacks on humans are rare.

According to veteran grizzly biologist Stephen Herrero (quoted in Hummel, 1991), "studies have shown that, even where grizzly bears have been shot and wounded, about three-quarters of the time they just try to get out of the way or go into cover."

Biologist Derek Stonorov (quoted in Walker, 1993), who has studied the coastal bears of Alaska for many years, says that "bears do not have a sinister personality . . . they aren't even particularly aggressive."

During three years of intensive grizzly study in the Khutzeymateen Valley of British Columbia, biologists learned to respect the restraint shown by the great bear. As the head biologist (MacHutchon, 1993) wrote, "Close encounters were common during the Khutzey-

Although actual attacks are rare, bear attacks inspire endless fascination. (Robert H. Busch)

mateen study (30 to 40 over three years) because of the nature of the work, but in no situation was a firearm essential."

Statistically, the chance of a grizzly attacking a human is very small. Grizzly researcher Steven French (quoted in Read, 1995) says that in terms of pure numbers, the number of grizzly attacks that kill humans "rank right up there with spontaneous human combustion."

In the last hundred years, fewer than 50 people in North America have lost their lives from grizzly attacks. About 150 attacks have been deemed serious in nature.

In the lower 48 states, only 14 people have died from grizzly attacks since 1900. In Alaska, despite a grizzly population of over 30,000 bears, only 24 fatalities from bear attacks have been recorded since the turn of the century. Almost half were hunters in remote parts of the state. As author Doug Peacock (1990) noted, "more people die of bad egg salad in a year than from grizzly attacks in a century."

Statistics do underline, however, the greater power of the grizzly compared to the black bear. In a recent study of bear injuries in British Columbia between 1960 and 1997 (Herrero and Higgins, *in press*), Stephen Herrero found that although there are 120,000 to 160,000 black bears in that province compared to 10,000 to 13,000 grizzlies, grizzlies inflicted about three times as many serious injuries and the same number of fatal injuries. Naturalist Andy Russell put it a bit more colorfully in his book *Grizzly Country* (1967): Comparing the two bears, he said, is like "standing a case of dynamite beside a sack of goose feathers."

When one considers that over a hundred people die *every day* in car accidents in North America, the number of bear kills should fade into proper perspective. But it doesn't. Each bear attack spawns a mass of sensational media coverage, which only magnifies the grizzly's already bad press.

The paranoia that accompanies a bear attack is both amazing and appalling. When one resident of Naknek, Alaska, was mauled by a female grizzly protecting her two cubs, furious townsfolk killed over a dozen innocent grizzlies in revenge.

One of the worst problems in grizzly country today is the sloppy security around most rural garbage dumps. Grizzlies feed at the dumps, learn to love the food, and learn not to fear the humans that bring additional goodies to their smelly buffet. Stephen Herrero stated in his classic book *Bear Attacks: Their Causes and Avoidance*

Garbage and bears are a combination that often leads to aggressive bears that have lost their fear of humans. (Robert H. Busch)

(1985), "Up to 1970, I calculated that inside the national parks, habituated, food-conditioned grizzlies were responsible for approximately two-thirds of all injuries inflicted on people."

The key phrase here is *"food-conditioned."* Two decades of experience at McNeil River State Game Sanctuary in Alaska have shown that grizzlies and humans can tolerate each other very well if the grizzlies have not learned to associate humans with easy food. Despite hundreds of human-bear encounters, sometimes at distances as close as 8 feet (3 m), not one person has ever been seriously harmed by a bear at McNeil River.

The problem comes when the territorial instinct in grizzlies breaks down in the face of excessive food left by sloppy humans. Unusual numbers of bears can be attracted to a single dump if the dump is not fenced, or if it does not use bear-proof containers for garbage. At the old Lake Louise dump in Alberta, I have counted as many as 17 of the great bears foraging at one time. The most famous of all garbage-eating grizzlies, though, were those at the Yellowstone National Park dumps.

Adolph Murie, writing in *A Naturalist in Alaska* in 1961, stated: "in a garbage dump in Yellowstone Park I have seen 30 grizzlies wallowing together with bodies practically touching."

For decades, tourists flocked to Yellowstone's garbage dumps to watch and photograph the bears. Park rangers actually encouraged the feeding. A. S. Johnson, writing in the February 1972 issue of *National Parks and Conservation,* recounted, "Bleacher seats were built; lights were furnished; garbage was even sorted for bears. One retired park employee recalls the distribution of edible garbage on 'tables,' [so] that visitors might have a better view of the bears as they fed." However, it finally became clear to park authorities that the attraction was creating dozens of problem bears.

John and Frank Craighead, two naturalists who had studied the park's bears since the 1950s, recommended phasing out the dumps over a ten-year period. Their recommendation was based on concerns that a rapid closing would cause the bears to stray widely in a desperate search for more garbage to feed upon. The Craigheads foresaw increased numbers of incidents of bears entering public campgrounds, and thus the potential for increased numbers of grizzlies to be shot.

However, park authorities disagreed and abruptly closed the dumps (the last one in Yellowstone was closed in 1971). The Craigheads' worst nightmare came true, as dozens of bears wandered into villages outside the park and marauded park campgrounds. Some were shot outside the park by hunters and ranchers. Others were killed by park rangers who feared that campers would be attacked. Although the exact numbers will never be known, it is likely that more than a hundred grizzlies lost their lives between 1968 and 1973 because of dump closures.

To make matters even worse, in Yellowstone and elsewhere, many park campsites were located beside scenic streams and ponds—a great place for camping, but also a perfect place for bears. To date, most parks have not rectified this oversight. Glacier National Park is one exception; campsites located in high-risk areas are now enclosed with tall chain-link fences. Still, your chance of a grizzly mauling in a park is less than one in a million.

One of the best-documented of grizzly attacks occurred in 1996, north of Yellowstone National Park. On November 8, hunting guide Joe Heimer took client Sonja Crowley on a trip to hunt trophy bull elk. Walking down a remote dirt road, they suddenly stumbled upon a sow grizzly with three cubs, a dangerous situation under any circumstances. The two backed up about 50 feet (15 m), but not soon enough.

The mother bear charged, running low to the ground, rattling her teeth and hissing. As the bear got close, Heimer raised his rifle and shot. He missed.

The bear hit him head on, knocking him on his back and sending his rifle flying. The angry sow bit into his right knee and then went for the left leg. Heimer grabbed the bear's upper lip in his fingers, shoving her back and squeezing as hard as he could.

Meanwhile, Crowley had moved toward the rifle, attracting the bear's attention. The sow dropped Heimer and took after Crowley, hitting her in the back and pushing her face into the snow. Then the sow sank her teeth into Crowley's head. The bear's bottom teeth went into the left side of Crowley's face, destroying part of her eye. The bear shook her and then started dragging her away. During all this time, Crowley was alive and lucid. "I could hear all the bones breaking as she bit down," she says (quoted in McMillion, 1998).

Heimer grabbed the rifle but couldn't take a shot, for fear of hitting Crowley. Suddenly the bear dropped Crowley and sprinted back to her cubs. Once she reassured herself that they were all right, she then wheeled and charged Heimer and Crowley again.

One more time, Heimer took careful aim and shot. The bear went down, but struggled to her feet. Heimer shot again, this time at point-blank range. The bear finally fell dead at his feet, and the horror was over.

The bear turned out to be bear Number 79, a 22-year-old matriarch well known to Yellowstone biologists. Whenever natural foods became too hard to find, bear Number 79 would amble into the civilized areas around the town of Gardiner and raid apple trees. First captured in 1981, bear Number 79 was repeatedly lured into culvert traps and relocated deep within the park. Until the attack in November, 1996, she hadn't hurt anyone, but little by little, her fear of humans was decreasing. As a result, she paid the ultimate price.

Heimer was stitched up later that night and was back to guiding within a week, but Crowley spent eight days in the hospital and lost most of her vision in one eye. Today, she has six steel plates holding her skull together, but she did survive.

However rare, grizzly attacks on humans do occur. You might accidentally come between a mother and her cub, happen upon a grizzly lying beside its kill, or you might just stumble on a bear napping in its day bed. You just don't know.

A grizzly's reaction in most of these situations is defensive in nature; actual intentional predation by grizzlies upon humans is extremely rare. The opposite is true for the black bear; most serious human injuries or deaths caused by black bears have been the result of predation.

Some grizzlies will charge; some will not. Frank Dufresne, a former director of the Alaska Game Commission, believed that only 1 grizzly in 25 will charge. British Columbia bear hunter James Gary Shelton has had about 50 close encounters with grizzlies; half of the bears ran away, and half acted aggressively.

Experience shows, however, that most grizzlies do not begin to lick their chops when they spot human intruders in their territory. Most bears will flee; in fact, most are long gone by the time the unsuspecting hiker or hunter blunders into their range.

Many early books on grizzlies declared that it was the unpredictable nature of the grizzly that made it a force to be reckoned with in the woods. Today, however, that attitude is changing. Jim Faro, a biologist with the Alaska Department of Fish and Game (quoted in Walker, 1993), says, "The term 'unpredictable' only means our knowledge is incomplete."

The average person's knowledge about grizzlies used to be based on hunting lore and fireside stories. Today, those fables and exaggerations are being replaced by fact, and more knowledge is emerging about how to act in grizzly country.

One of the most dangerous situations in bear country is the surprise close-range encounter, especially if the bear has cubs or is at a kill site. Steve Herrero, who reviewed bear attacks in British Columbia that occurred between 1960 and 1967 (Herrero and Higgins, *in press*), found that "of the serious or fatal grizzly bear incidents where

A head-on stare, with lowered ears, is often a sign of an anxious bear. A slow retreat might be in order before the bear charges. (Robert H. Busch)

Warning sign in bear country.

the bear's motivation could be inferred, 62 percent were categorized as involving a bear being startled at close range."

A few simple rules are in order. It is important to be alert in bear country: Watch for bear tracks, scat, day beds, diggings, overturned boulders, scratched trees, or rubbed trees. Any fresh signs should send up a red flag that it might be wise to back off. And if you smell rotting meat, do not investigate further; grizzlies defend their kills quickly and viciously. Watch for crows, ravens, and other birds that may be congregating near a kill site on the ground below.

Hikers should be careful to avoid high-risk areas such as game trails in thick brush or beside salmon streams. Other areas to avoid are avalanche chutes in spring and early summer, and burned-over areas where new clumps of forage plants are sprouting, all of which are favorite grizzly feeding areas.

In many cases, the decision the bear makes on attacking or not attacking depends on distance—the closer you are, the worse your chances. Therefore, if you spot a grizzly before it spots you, one of the best defenses is to back off and increase the distance between you.

Should a grizzly spot you in its territory, it is important not to run and to stay calm. As Doug Peacock (1990) recommends, "once [the bear] sees you, you had better stand dead still. Let him be dominant. Look off to one side and avoid eye contact."

However, a bear posturing with a lowered head and flattened ears, especially if it is chomping its jaws or slobbering, is clearly saying *Get out of my life*. A slow retreat might be in order before the bear charges. Never look the bear straight in the eyes.

Luckily, most charges are bluffs, moves intended to drive the intruder out of a bear's territory. Sadly, many hunters panic when charged, and many grizzlies needlessly are shot as a result. In fact, one recent book on bear attacks (written by a bear hunter) even recommends always shooting grizzlies whenever they are closer than 82 feet (25 m)—heavy-handed advice indeed.

If your worst nightmare comes true and you are attacked, do not try to run. If a strong tree is close by, you can try climbing it, but get as high as possible, for the bear will likely try to follow.

Opinions are mixed about whether you should drop your backpack while you back off. Some think it may give the grizzly something to attract its attention; others insist that you should keep the pack on, for it may protect your back if you are mauled.

A direct face-off, which preceded a bluff charge by this grizzly. (Robert H. Busch)

Once the bear is on top of you, playing dead seems to be the most recommended move. Cover your head with your arms and then either roll into a ball or try to keep your stomach flat to the ground. Then try to stay still and limp. The less you seem like struggling prey, the better.

This factor was recognized as early as 1806, when explorer Simon Fraser wrote of a native who was attacked by a grizzly: "she instantly laid down flat upon the ground and did not stir, in consequence of [which] the bear deserted [her]."

More recent corroboration of this advice comes from a tragic attack in 1976 in Glacier National Park. When a grizzly attacked one hiker, he resisted for a while and then played dead, placing his hands behind his head. Only then did the bear drop him and attack a second hiker, who resisted and was killed.

The exception to the rule of playing dead comes if you are attacked while sleeping outdoors. These attacks are not the result of a bear being surprised on the trail, defending cubs, or defending prey. Rather, this type of attack is the result of predation—often involving a bear that is looking for something to eat in a campground full of food smells. Some biologists believe that the flat-lying appearance of sleeping campers reminds the bear of wounded or dead prey lying on the ground.

Bears invading tents are usually looking for food. (Simulated tent break-in photographed with a captive grizzly, Fernandez & Peck/Adventure Photo & Film)

If you are attacked by a grizzly while you are lying on the ground or sleeping, you should fight back. As Stephen Herrero (1985) recommends, "Shout at the bear. Throw things at or near it so you can escape. Use every possible weapon or repellent you might have." Often the bear will get the message and will leave you with little more than a ripped tent and torn sleeping bag.

Opinions are mixed about the hot-pepper sprays currently available on the market as bear repellents. As Montana bear spray researcher Martin Smith (quoted in Turbak, 1984) says, "there will never be a repellent that will work with all the bears all the time."

IGBC BEAR PEPPER SPRAY POSITION PAPER

The following position paper is reproduced courtesy of the Interagency Grizzly Bear Committee [IGBC]:

Remember: bear pepper spray is not a substitute for following proper bear avoidance safety techniques.

- ◆ Selecting a bear pepper spray: Purchase only products that are clearly labeled "for deterring attacks by bears."

- ◆ Spray concentration should be 1.0 to 2.0 percent capsaicin and related capsaicinoids.

- ◆ Spray should be at least 225 grams or 7.9 ounces of net weight.

- ◆ Spray should be derived from Oleoresin of Capsicum (the IGBC Yellowstone Ecosystem Subcommittee recommends only oil-based 10 percent-plus oleoresin capsicum).

- ◆ Spray should be in a shotgun-cloud pattern.

- ◆ Spray should be delivered at a minimum range of 25 feet (7.6 m).

- ◆ Spray should last at least 6 seconds.

- ◆ Spray should be registered by the EPA (Environmental Protection Agency).[*]

---

[*]In November 1999, the EPA ordered the manufacturer of one bear spray to halt sales immediately because the product had used an unproven chemical, vanillyl pelargonamide, as the main ingredient.

When to use bear pepper spray:

- ♦ Bear pepper spray should be used as a deterrent only in an aggressive or attacking confrontation with a bear.
- ♦ Bear pepper spray is only effective when used as an airborne deterrent sprayed as a cloud at an aggressive animal. It should not be applied to people, tents, packs, other equipment, or surrounding area as a repellent.

How to use bear pepper spray:

Each person should carry a can of bear pepper spray when working or recreating in bear habitat. Spray should be carried in a quick, accessible fashion such as in a hip or chest holster. In your tent, keep bear pepper spray readily available next to your flashlight. You should also keep a can available in your cooking area. Spray should be tested once a year. Do not test spray in or near camping area. Be sure to check the expiration date on your can of bear spray.

- ♦ Remove safety clip.
- ♦ Aim slightly down and towards the approaching bear. If necessary, adjust for cross wind.
- ♦ Spray a brief shot when the bear is about 50 feet (15 m) away.
- ♦ Spray again if the bear continues to approach.
- ♦ Once the animal has retreated or is busy cleaning itself, leave the area as quickly as possible (don't run), or go to an immediate area of safety, such as a car, tree, or building.
- ♦ Do not chase or pursue the animal.

No deterrent is 100-percent effective, but compared to all others, including firearms, bear spray has demonstrated the most success in fending off threatening and attacking bears and preventing injury to the person and animal involved. The proper use of bear spray will reduce the number of grizzly bears killed in self-defense, reduce human injuries caused by bears, and help promote the recovery and survival of the grizzly bear.

Others are worried that the sprays might give some hikers a sense of false security, causing them to forget common sense in bear country. National Park warden Hal Morrison (quoted in Andreef, 1996) warns that "[bear spray is] just a tool to help," and is worried that some hikers may get the attitude that " 'I can whip any bear that I see.' . . . It's no substitute for common sense." Morrison himself has used the spray on a charging grizzly he encountered in Larch Valley near Banff, Alberta, a popular hiking area. "Most of it missed him but . . . the loud aerosol hiss deterred him," he says.

American hikers should note that it is illegal to bring sprays with Mace as the main ingredient, or sprays that are also intended for use on humans, into Canada.

The active ingredient in most bear sprays is not Mace but capsicum, which is derived from red peppers. This substance irritates the eyes and nasal passages of a bear, incapacitating it for about five minutes if it receives a direct blast. Bears get rid of the substance by rolling in wet grass or in water, and it causes no permanent damage.

Bear sprays were first developed in 1980 by American inventor Bill Pounds. They reached the market in 1986, under such macho names as *Standoff, Counter Assault, Assault Guard, Bear Guard, Bear Scare,* and many others.

Chuck Jonkel, an American bear biologist, knows of 15 incidents in which a bear spray may have prevented a serious black bear or grizzly attack. John Eisenhauer, a biologist involved in the development of *Standoff,* hopes that the spray may help condition problem bears to avoid humans.

In some cases, though, the opposite seems to be happening. Jim Hart, a conservation officer in Fort Nelson, British Columbia, has reported that some of the nuisance black bears in his area have been sprayed many times, and have become partially resistant to the spray.

Many people are concerned about the potential misuse of bear sprays. Wildlife photographer Michael Francis echoes the feelings of many: "People must be very careful with this spray and not push their luck in getting too close to bears just because they have the spray with them."

It is also important to remember that bear sprays can be used only at close quarters and can be blown away by wind. Many of the cans carry suggestions that you make sure the bear is downwind before spraying it, but few people have the time or presence of mind for such maneuvering in an attack situation.

Despite the IGBC recommendations on pp. 141–142, some experts do not recommend testing the can after purchasing it; there are many reports of cans slowly losing their pressure after such tests. And the spray cans have a limited volume, usually containing only enough spray for five or six two-second bursts. Many people now suggest carrying two cans, so that one can be used in each hand.

Opinions are also mixed on the use of flares against a charging grizzly. In some cases they have worked; in others, they haven't. In many cases, their use has resulted in accidental grass fires; as a result, in some areas, flares are banned.

The supposed advantages of wearing bear bells are a little more encouraging. In one study in Glacier National Park, only one hiker in four was found to be wearing bear bells, but of all the hikers charged by grizzlies, not one was carrying a bell. In dense brush, or near rushing water, however, the delicate sounds of bells may not be loud enough. Stephen Herrero (1985) loudly yodels in bear country, adding a "short, explosive high-pitched sound at the end." Other people have even carried airhorns into bear country, especially when they expected to encounter thick brush conditions.

Some outdoorsmen now suggest that all yodels or yells in bear country be repeated at least once, as many animals wait for a second sound before fleeing.

Hikers should note that a single high-pitched whistle is not recommended in alpine areas, as this sound is very similar to the call of the marmot and often attracts grizzlies. Unfortunately, many Canadian parks brochures still recommend using a sharp whistle, although the potential problems have been pointed out to them many times.

It is also recommended that hikers never go alone into grizzly country. Larger groups of people make more noise, and there is safety in numbers; in the case of an attack, your companions may be able to drive off a bear or summon help.

It is a good idea to avoid hiking at dusk or dawn, as these are times when bears actively feed.

Most authorities recommend that dogs never be taken into grizzly country, on the basis that a dog being chased by a bear might bring it right back to the dog's owner. However, I know of two cases in which dogs have driven off attacking grizzlies and I have heard of other cases in which just the sound of a barking dog was enough to scare off an inquisitive bear. Perhaps the best advice is to keep a dog on a leash if you wish, but don't let it run loose. Aside from keeping the dog out of bear trouble, a leash will also keep a dog from chasing or killing other wildlife.

If an aggressive bear or a bear that shows absolutely no fear of humans is encountered, report it as soon as possible to the nearest park warden or ranger. Most park officials take such reports very seriously, and will close hiking trails or campsites to prevent potential problems.

Besides making sure that bears know you're around, it is also wise to take simple precautions when camping in grizzly country:

♦ Avoid bringing strong-smelling meat such as bacon or fish into grizzly country. Try powdered or dried foods instead. Even the strong smell of wet socks can attract bears. (I once had a young black bear crawl into my tent, attracted by the pungent aroma of wet socks drying near a propane heater.)

♦ A clean camp means a bear-free camp; if you leave frozen bacon out to thaw overnight or forget to do the camp dishes, you might just have a very large visitor.

♦ All food and garbage should be kept in tight, airproof containers and suspended above a bear's reach. If your vehicle is nearby, lock the food in the trunk.

♦ Don't sleep in clothes that you've cooked in; to a bear, you'll smell like a giant hot dog in some strange kind of bun. It's also a good idea to sleep as far away from your cooking site as possible.

Most governments issue a wealth of public education materials on grizzlies. (Robert H. Busch)

♦ When you leave your campsite, burn all the garbage and then pack all of it out; burying it isn't good enough in bear country. Grizzlies have a tremendous sense of smell and the last thing you want is to get a bear used to eating human garbage.

♦ It is also a good idea to always sleep in a tent in grizzly country. There is some evidence that bears are more likely to attack a person sleeping out in the open.

Hunters must also take special care in grizzly country:

♦ Fresh meat should be suspended at least 10 feet (3 m) off the ground. (One Wyoming outfitter thoughtlessly left his meat in saddlebags packed onto his horse, which was tied to a tree. Both the meat and the horse were taken by a hungry grizzly.)

♦ Sleeping tents should be located well away from the meat.

♦ Gut piles should be burned, placed in airtight containers, and packed out.

♦ Hunters shouldn't hang around after a kill—fresh meat should be hauled out of grizzly country quickly, as the smell will attract bears from miles around.

In 1995, two hunters were mauled by a sow grizzly and her two cubs when they found the men field dressing an elk they had shot near

Studies have observed that females with cubs to protect are responsible for the majority of grizzly attacks. (Mark Newman/Adventure Photo & Film)

Albert River, British Columbia. Both men died. Hunters should also be alert when hiking out with the meat; to a hungry grizzly, a hunter with a backpack full of meat is just an appetizing entrée on two legs.

Which are the most dangerous grizzlies? Studies show that females with cubs are probably at the top of the list. One research study found that in a bear population in which only 17 percent of the animals were females with cubs, almost 80 percent of the human injuries caused by bears were caused by those females. In Stephen Herrero's exhaustive study of 279 grizzly–human encounters, 74 percent involved female grizzlies with cubs. In a review of British Columbia bear attacks that occurred between 1960 and 1997, adult females were identified in 79 percent of the incidents (Herrero and Higgins, *in press*).

Subadult bears, which are both stressed by being driven off by their mothers and have not yet learned to fear humans, also often cause trouble: Like teenaged humans, they tend to be both fearless and reckless. Half of all the fatal maulings in Glacier National Park have been by subadult grizzlies.

Statistically, September seems to be the worst month for grizzly attacks. Grizzlies in the fall must eat huge volumes of food in preparation for winter, and the desperate search for food seems to make bears incautious and aggressive. Half of all the fatal maulings of humans by grizzlies in Glacier National Park in the past 30 years have occurred in September.

September 1995 was a particularly bad month. In the first part of the month, a Helena, Montana, man named Lester Ashwood was mauled by a grizzly in Glacier National Park. On September 19, 1995, 18-year-old Bram Schaffer was badly mauled by a big sow grizzly about 10 miles (15 km) north of Yellowstone National Park. About a week later, another big female grizzly marauded a campground at Lake Louise in Alberta, mauling six tourists.

There is some evidence that the smell of human blood, detectable by bears in menstruating women, may attract curious bears, although some grizzly biologists do not believe this has been well documented. Similarly, the smell of perfumes and colognes might cause curious grizzlies to approach humans closer than they normally would. Lightning and thunderstorms may also disturb bears and cause unnatural behaviour.

In August 1967, on the famous "Night of the Grizzlies," when two young women were killed by two different grizzlies in two different areas of Glacier National Park, a number of these tragic factors all came into play on one terrible night.

First, the summer of 1967 was unusually hot and dry, with over a hundred lightning strikes in the Park, which may have agitated the bears. The hot weather resulted in a poor berry crop and the bears soon learned to steal food from fishing camps and garbage dumps.

The second major factor was alleged mismanagement on the part of park wardens. For three months prior to the fatal mauling of a young woman near Trout Lake, fishermen and hikers had lodged dozens of complaints about a very thin, unusually aggressive grizzly. Their complaints were ignored.

In the case of the young woman who was mauled in the Granite Park Campground on the same night, several more serious errors were made by park employees. For months prior to the attack, employees had been hauling garbage out to an open pit behind the Granite Park Chalet, where foraging grizzlies each night had become quite a tourist attraction. This was a blatant violation of park policy, but like many rules, this one was ignored. The campground was located smack in the middle of an area that had been frequented by grizzlies for at least ten years, and yet few people recognized the dangers. Worse yet, the Granite Park Campground was less than 200 yards (183 m) from the garbage dump itself.

After the Granite Park Campground mauling, park wardens were dispatched into the area with orders to kill every grizzly on sight, a heavy-handed procedure which resulted in the shootings of three innocent grizzlies. Autopsies of the three bears showed that none were responsible for the mauling.

Tragically, one of the bears was a mother with two cubs. A park official tried to shoot one of the cubs and succeeded in only wounding it, blowing away part of its jaw. Unbelievably, although both orphaned cubs stayed around the area for a long time, insufficient effort was put into catching them or ending their suffering. A year later, the wounded cub was spotted; it was in poor condition because it could not feed properly. A park ranger finally put the poor animal out of its misery. The fate of the other cub is unknown. The bear responsible for the fatal mauling at the Granite Park Campground was never positively identified.

After the two maulings in 1967, Glacier National Park officials instituted a long list of common-sense measures to prevent further bear–human problems. Trails were closed down at the first report of grizzlies in the area. Open garbage dumps were closed, and rangers enforced a strict "pack in, pack out" garbage policy for hikers and fishermen. Information booklets were distributed to educate back-country users. And all problem bears that bothered a human more than once were shot immediately.

All backcountry users would do well to heed the sage advice of grizzly expert Stephen Herrero, who wrote in *Bear Attacks: Their Causes and Avoidance* (1985), "Your best weapon to minimize the risk of a bear attack is your brain."

CHAPTER

6

The Future of the Grizzly

Space is air for the great beasts who roam the earth. Now is their final breath.

JOHN WEAVER, 1991

HABITAT LOSS AND LOGGING

Like every other North American predator, the grizzly has suffered tremendously from loss of habitat. As Aldo Leopold wrote so eloquently in *A Sand County Almanac,* "Permanent grizzly ranges and permanent wilderness areas are, of course, two names for one problem. Enthusiasm about either requires a long view of conservation, and a historical perspective."

Although the spread of rural settlements, ranches, oil and gas developments, mining, and other backcountry uses have all destroyed some grizzly habitat, the most pervasive threat across the continent is likely habitat loss due to clearcut logging.

Loggers are quick to point out that clearcutting does provide some short-term benefits to grizzlies, such as the growth of new grasses and low-lying berry bushes on newly cut blocks.

However, according to the B.C. Wildlife Branch, "most of the benefits associated with timber harvesting are negated by the intensive land use and management that follows." Tony Hamilton, a bear biologist with the B.C. Wildlife Branch, believes that the provincial grizzly population is on the decline and that one of the most significant factors in the decline is logging. "Clearcutting," says Hamilton, "continues to be concentrated in bear habitats."

In a 1987 study in southeastern Alaska, biologist J. W. Schoen found that 88 percent of old-growth forest grizzly dens occurred within commercial timber stands.

Habitat loss is the worst threat facing the grizzly. (Robert H. Busch)

Logging companies must build roads to harvest and remove the trees, but the result is increased access to grizzlies by hunters and poachers, as well as direct loss of old-growth forest tracts. Studies have shown that old-growth forests provide not only potential den sites, but also crucial thermal cover to grizzlies.

After an area is clearcut, foresters often use herbicides to control the growth of unwanted vegetation. Unfortunately, all too often, the new vegetation is just what grizzlies thrive on—berries, devil's club, skunk cabbage, and other forage plants.

In 1991, a B.C. Environment study headed by Tony Hamilton found that the use of herbicides can seriously affect the availability of grizzly foods over both the long and short terms. Over the short term, the grizzly's food supplies can be seriously reduced through the killing of vegetation. Over the long haul, dense stands of new trees can rob berry bushes and other low vegetative growth of the sun they need to survive. Very few of the grizzly's favorite foods can thrive under low-light conditions.

In response to queries on how to reduce the damage that logging has done to bear habitat, the World Wildlife Fund has made the following suggestions:

♦ Leave ½-mile (0.8-km) strips on both sides of streams and rivers.

♦ Avoid intensive feeding areas like avalanche chutes and grassy meadows.

♦ Leave corridors of cover along roads and close others altogether after logging, to reduce the poaching that often follows the introduction of new roads in remote areas.

♦ Use selective logging wherever possible as an alternative to clearcutting, or leave islands of trees in cuts larger than 20 acres (8 hectares).

♦ Follow strict procedures for garbage disposal.

It is distressing that in many parts of western North America, these guidelines and similar regulations have been blithely ignored by logging companies that are in too much of a rush to make a quick buck.

In my first three years of living in a remote area of central British Columbia, I saw numerous incidences of improper garbage disposal by loggers, "controlled" burns that soon got out of control due to inadequate supervision, illegal clearcuts taken right to the edge of critical salmon streams, improperly prepared logging roads, and flagrant violations of replanting regulations. All of these types of infractions could have negative impacts on grizzly populations.

ROAD ACCESS

In addition to clearcutting, the invasion of roads into grizzly territory has been one of the major factors leading to their decline. Roads provide access for all sorts of human activities, most of which negatively affect bears.

Roads dissect and partition bear habitats, cause direct mortalities through collisions with vehicles, and cause indirect mortalities through illegal kills and poaching. As bear biologist Rob Wielgus (quoted in Hummel, 1991) points out, "It's not roads that kill bears, it's people travelling on the roads with guns that kill bears."

Bears may also be attracted to roadsides seeded in lush new grasses, increasing the potential for legal and illegal shooting.

A 1992 study by biologist J. W. Schoen found that the total number of grizzlies killed on part of Alaska's Chichagof Island was proportional to the road density. In Alberta's Eastern Slopes Grizzly Project, 85 percent of 462 human-caused deaths occurred within 1,640 feet (500 m) of a road.

AGRICULTURE AND RANCHING

Agricultural and ranching activities have not only destroyed grizzly habitat directly, but have also affected the big bear indirectly because of poor husbandry practices and general intolerance of predators.

The practice of grazing cattle and sheep in high alpine and subalpine valleys is particularly distressing, because these slopes constitute important feeding habitats for grizzlies in the spring and fall. These areas also contain delicate vegetation that is quickly destroyed by the trampling of hundreds of hooves.

In addition, most high-capability farmland is concentrated in valley bottoms that are also excellent habitat for grizzlies. The result is

Although the grizzly is hated by many ranchers, actual losses of livestock to grizzlies are small. When a bear is found over a livestock carcass, it is often wrongfully blamed for the kill. (Robert H. Busch)

that grizzlies are pushed higher and higher away from good land to less attractive but more remote mountainous areas where neither farming nor ranching is practical, and where life is tough, even for a grizzly.

PETROLEUM AND MINING EXPLORATION

Much of the devastation caused by oil and gas ventures or mining activities occurs in the exploratory stages, when the impact of surface trenching, the cutting of seismic lines, clearing for access roads, and human settlements around mining camps or oil and gas fields is felt. Ecologically fragile areas can take centuries to recover from such disturbances, which may result in a migration of grizzlies out of the area altogether.

Oil exploration, such as this well in northern Alberta, has invaded many areas of wilderness, leaving behind both garbage and access roads, both of which are bad for grizzlies. (Robert H. Busch)

HYDROELECTRIC DEVELOPMENT

Although we all take hydroelectric development and its benefits for granted, consider the effects of hydropower lines and dams on grizzlies.

In many areas across the western half of North America, huge dam developments have resulted in flooded valleys and destroyed salmon runs. Valley bottoms are key grizzly habitats. Salmon, of course, is a favorite food of the grizzly and a crucial source of protein in the months prior to hibernation.

There has also been significant direct bear habitat loss due to the cutting of hydro lines across grizzly terrain, as well as indirect habitat loss from weed and brush control programs along hydro rights of way. And all too often, these rights of way become access routes for back-

When pristine rivers such as this are dammed for hydroelectric power, riparian wildlife often suffers. (Robert H. Busch)

country users who use ATVs, skis, or snowmobiles in what once was wilderness.

BACKCOUNTRY DEVELOPMENT

Backcountry development includes a wide variety of usages of re-mote lands, ranging from the relatively benign effects of lone cross-country skiers to the devastating effects of huge megaresorts.

These large developments, which may include alpine villages, golf courses, and ski hills, all produce bear problems not only due to direct habitat loss but also due to the access and garbage they provide. A growing number of ski resorts are now turning into year-round resorts, which expands exponentially the negative affects they have

Vacation cabins often lead to conflicts with bears resulting from improper disposal of garbage. (Robert H. Busch)

on grizzly populations. And both increased access and increased amounts of garbage mean increased numbers of dead bears.

Urbanites with cabins in backcountry can reduce their effects on grizzlies primarily through proper handling of garbage. Even such innocuous acts as leaving garbage or pet food outside the back door or on decks can cause serious problems in grizzly country.

Developers can minimize effects on grizzlies by avoiding crucial habitats such as riparian zones and meadows, by leaving strips of cover along roads and waterways, and by enforcing proper garbage-handling procedures. A little thought in planning can mean life or death to the area's resident grizzlies.

The cumulative effects of rural settlements, recreational use, mining and hydrocarbon exploration, and other human factors have pushed the great grizzly to the edge of its existence.

In February 2000, a report by Stephen Herrero, leader of the Eastern Slopes Grizzly Bear Project, predicted a dangerous decline in the number of grizzlies in the central Rocky Mountains of Alberta and British Columbia if human activities are not curtailed. The report indicated that without additional management practices, the number of grizzlies in Kananaskis Country and Banff National Park could be cut by 40 to 50 percent over the next 20 years. The current grizzly population estimates are 35 to 50 grizzlies in Kananaskis Country, a recreation area northwest of Calgary, and 55 to 80 grizzlies in Banff National Park.

"We need to manage the amount of human contact in the whole system if we want to maintain grizzly bears," said Herrero (quoted in "Grizzlies in danger," 2000). "All things being equal, [grizzly] mortality is directly related to the number of encounters between bears and people."

Those same ominous words could well be applied to all the grizzlies left on this continent.

THE ROLE OF PARKS

One might think that parks are the answer to the threat of habitat loss. However, the preservation of grizzlies and other large predators

Parks can act as reserves for bears, but many bears are shot when they stray outside park boundaries. (Robert H. Busch)

in parks and reserves cannot be guaranteed, for the simple reason that animals do not respect political boundaries. A study of 12 resident grizzlies in British Columbia's Yoho National Park determined that when 9 of these bears left the park, they were all shot within a year. Yoho is now trying to save its grizzlies by closing several key areas in the park to humans, in order to let the bears rebuild their numbers.

One answer to this tragic loss of life is to establish no-hunting buffer zones around such parks. This has been done recently in the case of the Khutzeymateen Provincial Park in northwest British Columbia. Another is to add additional reserves as refuges for grizzlies. And still another solution is to stop the legal hunting of grizzlies, which is still allowed in some provincial parks. Currently, hunting is allowed in 20 of Canada's 53 largest provincial parks.

One Canadian park with a substantial grizzly population is Alberta's Jasper National Park, which over a hundred grizzlies call home. The park's grizzly population has decreased by half since the 1950s due to hunting just outside the park, losses from poaching, and "nuisance" kills. Between 1951 and 1989, 17 park bears died from highway or railway accidents. Nine others were killed as nuisance bears.

Alberta's Banff National Park is currently home to between 55 and 80 grizzlies. Unfortunately, the park is also home to hundreds of human residents and attracts thousands of summer and winter tourists. Grizzlies regularly prowled the northern wooded outskirts of the town of Banff, and on the slopes above the town, some excellent alpine grizzly habitat was sliced into ski runs. Conflicts between the two-legged and four-legged residents of the park were rampant until the mid-1990s, when conservationists demanded that something be done.

In 1994, the future of Banff National Park's grizzlies took a turn for the better when the Ministry of Canadian Heritage announced the formation of the Banff-Bow Valley Task Force, whose job was to assess future environmental impacts upon the park and its resident animals. The Eastern Slopes Grizzly Project reported to the task force specifically on the projected future impacts on grizzlies.

In 1996, the task force's final report recommended many steps that provided some hope for the future of the Banff grizzlies. The report decreed that no new park lands would be leased for commercial development. The Banff airstrip and army cadet camp would be removed. Fences around Banff will help separate the people from the bears, reducing the bears' access to local garbage. And an education program will help raise bear awareness among residents and visitors.

Since 1971, 77 grizzlies are known to have died within Banff National Park as a result of encounters with humans. Many were killed as nuisance or problem bears. Ten were killed by collisions with cars, trucks, or trains. The total annual mortality rate is between 3 and 6 percent. Grizzly biologist Stephen Herrero (quoted in Legault, 1996) says that this rate is still too high. "One percent is the maximum the Banff [grizzly] population can maintain," he says.

America's oldest national park, Yellowstone, became a haven for grizzlies in 1872. It now holds well over 200 bears, which sounds like a comfortable number. However, many think that the park may still become an island of extinction. A 1989 Montana State University study bluntly stated: "The Yellowstone grizzly population is doomed to extinction."

However, Yellowstone National Park authorities rose to the challenge. As Yellowstone bear biologist Dave Mattson (quoted in Legault, 1996) says, "the way to reduce bear mortality is to reduce contact with people." And so, Yellowstone officials limited and controlled backcountry use, cleaned up garbage problems, prohibited feeding of bears by tourists, cleaned up the campsites, and began to use bearproof trash cans. By the early 1990s, their efforts had paid

Many parks, such as Wells Gray Provincial Park in British Columbia, post no-feeding signs to educate the public of the dangers of feeding bears. (Robert H. Busch)

off, and the grizzly population in Yellowstone has now apparently stabilized.

The Yellowstone grizzlies are still not out of trouble, though. The human population around Yellowstone National Park is expected to double within 30 years. As Chuck Schwartz, a park official (quoted in Wilkinson, 2000), says, "For a Yellowstone grizzly, the chances are slim that it can exist without stumbling into trouble—whether it's a hunter, a hiker, a cow, a highway, a tourist development, or a subdivision."

Moreover, Yellowstone grizzlies face potential food shortages due to a number of unrelated factors. Firstly, blister rust disease is currently harming the whitepark pine stands, potentially decreasing the number of whitebark pine cones for the grizzlies to feed upon. Secondly, introduced lake trout (a deepwater fish that grizzlies normally can't catch) in Yellowstone Lake are devouring the local cutthroat trout, which spawn in shallow water and are a favorite spring food for Yellowstone grizzlies. And lastly, if the pervasive effects attributed to global warming continue, the ranges of both whitebark pines and cutworm moths may decrease, again depleting two major bear food sources.

Another problem facing many parks today is the looming threat of legal actions. In 1972, a grizzly in Yellowstone National Park killed a young camper named Harry Walker. Walker's parents promptly sued the National Park Service. The Park Service's lawyers argued that Walker had been sloppy with his garbage and been camped illegally, but Judge A. Andrew Hauk found the National Park Service liable for a whopping $87,417 in damages. Although the decision was later reversed on legal technicalities, it sent shockwaves through the park services on both sides of the Canada–United States border, who now fear similar actions as a result of their wild charges.

POACHING

Quite predictably, the effect of humans on grizzlies is often negative. Grizzlies can readily live alongside man with few problems, but some humans like to end the relationship with a bang. And many on the end of the gun these days are poachers looking for bear parts.

The international trade in bear parts is a growing problem with its roots deep in Asian culture. Bear cubs are sold in some Asian countries for $1,600 to $5,000. When they reach adulthood, they are killed for the parts of their body that are used in traditional Asian medicine.

Bear gall bladders are in particular demand, with special farms now set up in Asia that raise bears and then "'milk" them of their gall.

To the Chinese, bear gall bladders are known as *fel ursi,* and are used to treat fevers, convulsions, all types of pain, and even hemorrhoids. Gall bladders produce a bile that contains a chemical called ursodeoxycholic acid, or UDCA, which may actually have some medicinal properties. Contrary to popular Asian mythology, though, UDCA is not an effective aphrodisiac, and nor does it cure cancer.

The bladders are usually crushed to a powder, which is then mixed with other animal parts or herbs. The demand for the bladders is staggering. One Canadian buyer alone purchased 1,125 bear gall bladders in less than a year. Currently, black-market gall bladders can be purchased in Vancouver for about $1,000 each. Gall bladders are in such demand that a single bladder can reach up to $55,000 in Korea, making the business highly lucrative.

Korea has one of the worst records for inhumane treatment of bears in all of the world. As recently as the early 1990s, many reports came out of Korea of live bears being bludgeoned to death in front of customers in restaurants in order to prove that the meat was fresh. And when Seoul hosted the 1988 Olympic Games, 30 sun bears were smuggled into the country and slaughtered to feed the Korean athletes.

Another popular bear part is the paw, which is used in soup. Hunters are paid about $60 per paw. Wholesalers then pay about $100 each and resell them to restaurants for about $200 each. Prepared in a fancy dish at a good restaurant in Tokyo, a bowl of bear-paw soup may go for $850.

Other bear parts are also in high demand. Bear claws can sell for up to $10 each, bear teeth for $60 each, and skulls for $75 each. An entire trophy grizzly can go for up to $10,000.

There is a booming market for grizzly heads and hides that are used as trophy mounts, purchased illegally for someone's den or wall. Years ago, I saw a large grizzly head for sale in a taxidermy shop in northern Montana and when I inquired as to where the head had been acquired, I was told by the proprietor, "You don't want to know and I don't want to say."

The magnitude of the grizzly poaching problem in North America is very difficult to quantify. However, some idea can be gained from the fact that when author Timothy Treadwell was researching his book *Among Grizzlies,* he talked to a poacher who admitted taking over a thousand grizzlies illegally in southern Alaska. If one man can be responsible for such a slaughter, think what the total for the continent must be. And even when a poacher is caught and convicted, nothing can bring back the dead bears.

In October 1995, a grizzly carcass was found near Quesnel, British Columbia, with only the penis bone (baculum) missing. Ground up and used in potions, the bone is prized in Chinese medicine as an aphrodisiac. The incident sums up the shocking magnitude of the poaching problem: an entire grizzly killed just for one small bone destined to boost the love life of some elderly Asian.

Because of the lucrative nature of the trade, several Asian bear species are seriously threatened. As a result, there is increasing pressure on North American bear populations.

However, it is thought that the rarity of the grizzly has sheltered it somewhat from poachers compared to the thousands of black bears illegally killed each year.

It is estimated that about 40,000 black bears are poached each year in the United States. There is no similar estimate for the grizzly.

GRIZZLY WATCHING

In recent years, ecotourism has boomed, as increasing numbers of people travel to see wild places and wild species. According to the United States Fish and Wildlife Service, from 1980 to 1995, the number of people who traveled to watch wildlife increased by 63 percent, almost four times the national growth rate.

In the early 1990s, the ecotourism market grew 30 percent each year, according to the World Tourism Organization.

At Alaska's Katmai National Park, the number of visitors increased from 11,000 in 1981 to 50,000 in 1991, a five-fold increase in just ten years.

The most famous of bear-watching sites is at McNeil River, on the coast of Alaska southwest of Anchorage. As the river flows out of the mountains down the coast into Kamishak Bay, it tumbles over a series of rock ledges, creating a series of falls and pools. During late summer and early fall, spawning chum and chinook salmon accumulate in the pools, along with the world's largest concentration of griz-

The grizzly's appeal makes it a popular tourist attraction. (Jean Capps/Dragonsnaps)

zlies. Up to 67 grizzlies have been counted at the main falls at one time. In total, about 120 to 150 grizzlies visit the sanctuary from June through September.

In 1955, pressure from conservationists resulted in the entire drainage being closed to bear hunting. Four years later, when Alaska gained statehood, the McNeil River Reserve was changed to the

McNeil River Falls, home of the greatest concentration of grizzlies in the world. (Karl Sommerer)

McNeil River Closed Area. In 1967, it became the McNeil River State Game Sanctuary. The entire McNeil River drainage, lower 6 miles (9 km) of the Paint River drainage, nearby Mikfik Creek, and all drainages into McNeil Cove are completely closed to all hunting today.

The sanctuary had only 5 visitors in 1968. Currently, almost 2,000 people per year apply for 140 permits, which are drawn by the Alaska Department of Fish and Game. The permits are good for only four days each. Permit applications cost $20 and must be submitted by March 15. The permit system has been in place since 1997.

The original sanctuary had few rules. "We had people running up and down both sides of the river. There were even people fishing at the falls, right where the bears feed. It was crazy," says regional fish and wildlife manager Jim Faro (quoted in Sherwonit, 1996). Visitor controls were finally put in place in 1973.

Today, groups of no more than 10 people are escorted at low tide to the falls where the bears gorge on salmon. Prior to the July–August chum and chinook spawning season, the McNeil bears can be found at nearby Mikfik Creek, where they dine on early sockeye runs and rich vegetation (see p. 171).

At both areas, grizzlies feed, fight, mate, and nurse within only a few feet of awestruck humans.

In 1991, Alaska added 30,000 acres (12,146 hectares) around Paint River, north of the sanctuary, and a small area south of the sanctuary, to the original 85,000 acres (34,413 hectares).

A chunk of land to the north of the sanctuary was designated the McNeil River State Game Refuge. Unfortunately for the bears, hunting is allowed in the refuge.

McNeil River provides an example of just how accomodating the grizzly can be to the presence of humans. During all of its years of existence as a game refuge, only 2 people have been hurt. In 1955, a bear bit a man on the foot. However, eyewitness Steve McCutcheon (quoted in Walker, 1993) says "that was because the fellow stepped on her."

In 1958, a man got between a sow and her new cubs. The bear charged immediately. According to Clem Tillion, a local guide (quoted in Walker, 1993), "He tripped and fell, and she ran right over him, her claws tearing a nasty wound from knee to hip . . . it really wasn't an attack."

Other spots around Alaska are also becoming well known for grizzly watching. Pack Creek, in the Stan Price State Wildlife Sanctuary

This bear appears to be waving to his audience at McNeil River, Alaska. (Karl Sommerer)

southwest of Juneau on Admiralty Island, is a site where 20 to 30 bears can be seen at one time. The island is home to about 1,500 grizzlies that grow fat on salmon runs each summer and fall. In fact, the island was known to early natives as *Kootznoowoo*, meaning "fortress of bears."

Permits are required to view bears at Pack Creek between June 1 and September 10. Daily visits are limited to 24 lucky humans during the peak viewing time between July 5 and August 25. The area is co-managed by the Alaska Department of Fish and Game and the U.S. Forest Service.

On Kodiak Island, the 1.6 million-acre (0.6 million-hectare) Kodiak Island National Wildlife Refuge takes up about two-thirds of the island and is home to a dense concentration of bears. There may be as many as 2,500 bears in the refuge.

Established in 1941, the Refuge is famous for high numbers of bears along the O'Malley River. The river is only 800 yards (732 meters) long and links Karluk Lake and O'Malley Lake. From June through November, a flood of spawning salmon draws about 130 bears to the site. A wooden viewing platform along the river provides a ringside seat for the lucky bear-watchers, who are chosen by lottery. Fraser River is another good bear-watching site on the same island.

Brooks River Falls and Camp, within Katmai National Park and Preserve, is another prime bear-watching spot. In July, salmon gathering below a 6-foot (2-m) falls attract dozens of big bears. Although no special permits are required, a $10-per-day user fee is charged at the site. About 600 grizzlies roam Katmai National Park and Preserve, which is located just west of McNeil River.

Denali National Park and Preserve is well known for its light-colored "Toklat" grizzlies. Although private vehicles are not allowed in the park, shuttle buses travel a spectacular road where grazing grizzlies are often seen. Visitors who are seeking more of an adventure can apply to the park superintendent for an overnight backpacking permit. About 90 percent of visitors to Denali do see a grizzly.

Yellowstone National Park, despite its overdevelopment, is also a good spot to watch grizzlies. The best sites are along the road between Canyon and Fishing Bridges, from Mount Washburn, and in the Lamar Valley in the northeast corner of the park.

In Canada, there are many grizzly-watching sites. Two are especially notable. The Khutzeymateen River, on the coast 50 miles (91 km) northwest of Prince Rupert, British Columbia, is host to about 60 bears each spring. About 171 square miles (443 square km) of the valley are now preserved, but the fight to preserve the valley's bears was not an easy one.

Aside from two tiny native reserve parcels, which had been logged in 1950 and 1956, the valley had remained in a pristine condi-

Khutzeymateen Provincial Park is home to 50 or 60 grizzlies, and is Canada's first grizzly preserve. (Dan Wakeman)

tion until 1983, when a logging company applied to log part of the valley. The B.C. Forest Service approved the application, on the condition that a land-use plan stating the effects upon the valley's grizzlies be drafted first.

In 1985, many logging plans across the province were put on hold, as the government's Wilderness Advisory Committee began to analyze land-use conflicts that had set conservationists against loggers. A year later, the Committee recommended that the valley's grizzlies and their habitat be studied further.

In 1988, the Minister of Forests and the Minister of Environment, Lands, and Parks established a joint study aimed at determining the impact of timber harvesting in the Khutzeymateen Valley on grizzlies. The three-year study combined radio-collaring of 20 grizzlies, trapping, direct observation, detection at radio-controlled camera sites, and aerial surveys.

The study released its final report in May 1992. The report stated unequivocally that "forestry development in the Khutzeymateen will result in an immediate and long-term reduction in the capability of the habitat to support grizzly bears."

The provincial government heeded the report's recommendations, and in late 1992 announced the creation of Canada's first grizzly bear preserve, Khutzeymateen Provincial Park.

The rich sedges along the Khutzeymateen River in British Columbia attract many grizzlies each spring. (Dan Wakeman)

Today, ecotours along the Khutzeymateen River and nearby estuary take place from May through June, when the bears are feeding on sedges along the inlet. The Khutzeymateen's river system also supports four species of salmon, making it even more attractive to the big bears.

Further south along the B.C. coast, the Knight Inlet Lodge floats in pristine Knight Inlet. Accessible only by floatplane or boat, the lodge plays host to tourists who watch grizzlies fishing for salmon in late August in an artificial spawning channel or foraging along the inlet in the spring. A maximum of 10 people are taken to view the bears at once.

Up to 40 bears gather within a few miles of the lodge when the salmon are running up the Glendale River. The lodge has erected five elevated viewing platforms in three areas.

Other good spots in Canada for spotting grizzlies are in the Kitlope area of British Columbia, which is the largest intact coastal rainforest in all of North America, the huge Tatshenshini Park in the northwest corner of the province, and the Bella Coola to Atnarko River stretch in west-central British Columbia. All of these areas are quite undeveloped, with little in the way of tourist facilities.

The Tatshenshini-Alsek Provincial Park is especially spectacular. It abuts the Yukon's Kluane National Park Reserve and Alaska's Glacier National Park, making the area one of the largest preserved blocks of wilderness in the world.

In 1996, the B.C. provincial government enhanced the grizzly's future in the Bella Coola-Atnarko area by purchasing 254 acres (103 hectares) of privately owned land near the junction of the Atnarko and Talchako rivers in Tweedsmuir Provincial Park. The land had originally been slated for logging, to be followed by recreational or residential development.

The area's salmon runs attract grizzlies from as far as 86 miles (130 km) away. When the salmon are spawning, up to 50 grizzlies can be found in the area, which also contains First Nations archeological sites and pristine old-growth forests.

At all of these sites, the awesome experience of watching bears only a short distance away is something never to be forgotten. Canadian wildlife photographer Karl Sommerer visited Mikfik Creek in the McNeil River sanctuary in 1992 and is still awestruck: "Bears growling and howling, chasing and fighting, mixed sounds from the creek, gulls and bald eagles, the ever-present danger made this an unforgetable event." (Sommerer, personal communication, 2000)

Shoulder to shoulder grizzlies are common only at rich feeding sites such as Mikfik Creek in Alaska. (Karl Sommerer)

Ecotourism has its critics, however. Humans must be careful, for example, not to disturb bears unduly. Even at McNeil River, where viewing is carefully controlled, there are a few bears that have never learned to trust humans and emerge only at night to feed, obviously stressed by the close interactions with humans.

These tourists are far too close to this mother grizzly and her cubs in southern Alaska. (Robert McCaw)

171

There is also the constant danger of habituation leading to a loss of a bear's natural fear of humans. Some of these bears may become food-conditioned; once they learn to live off human garbage, these areas may have all the problems associated with garbage bears. Other bears may, through their loss of fear, learn to feed along roads or near towns. Because of the lack of human tolerance for grizzlies in close proximity, these bears may end up being killed.

However, as long as grizzly-watching is closely controlled, the benefits probably outweigh the potential problems. According to McNeil River sanctuary manager Larry Aumiller (quoted in Walker, 1993), grizzly-watching creates "a bond between people and the bear that they are watching. This can only help bears in the long run."

RESEARCH

Bear research has come a long way since the early days, when biologists wrestled black bears to the ground to place an ether-filled cone over their muzzles. That was the state of the art as far as field biology went in the 1950s. Today, things are different.

In the early 1950s, one of the biggest problems was tranquilizing the bears. Early drugs such as succinylcholine chloride (sucostrin) and M-99 often proved fatal to bears. Today, drugs such as ketamine hydrochloride and xylazine are safer alternatives, administered by jab sticks or from specially designed rifles.

After the bear is tranquilized, its eyes are dabbed with ointment and the face is covered with cloth or a bag, to prevent the eyes from drying out while the animal is being examined.

In a typical examination, the animal is weighed, measured, and the heart rate, respiration rate, and anal temperature are taken. A premolar tooth is removed, to be sectioned for aging the bear. A bit of fur may be clipped off for DNA analysis to determine familial relationships. A tiny amount of blood may be drawn to check the animal's overall health and to search for microscopic parasites. Using a metal punch, biologists often affix plastic or metal ear tags that will help researchers or wildlife managers identify the animal from afar later on.

The last task before the bear is released is usually to attach a radio-collar. The collar itself may be made of canvas or neoprene, with rivets or screws that hold the collar on the bear. Attached to the radio-collar is a tiny transmitter and battery, sealed in a waterproof

Attaching a radio-collar to a tranquilized bear on the coast of British Columbia. (E. C. Lofroth/B.C. Wildlife Branch)

case. The antenna of the transmitter is often sewn between the layers of the collar, or else projects a few inches behind the collar.

The beeping signals emitted by the radio transmitters can be picked up by receivers many miles away, depending on terrain. "Trees, bumps, hills, gullies; all these really affect the signal," says grizzly researcher Bruce McLellan (quoted in Domico, 1988). "If I

These biologists are measuring the heart girth of a tranquilized bear in British Columbia. (E. C. Lofroth/B.C. Wildlife Branch)

can get a reading as far [away] as 5 or 6 miles (8 to 10 kilometers), then I feel we're doing good."

The canvas strap of the collar can be designed to rot and fall off within a certain period of time. Motion-sensitive collars can be used that tell researchers when the bear is not moving.

This new technology has been responsible for a veritable explosion in the grizzly database, especially of information that could not possibly have been gathered even 20 years ago. In 1997, Alberta biologist Charles Mamo discovered that ten grizzlies, including females and cubs, were using the Lake Louise ski hill slopes at night, a crucial discovery for management of the area. "If not for radio telemetry," says Mamo (quoted in Marty, 1997), "we would not have known they were there at all."

Like all field research, grizzly research is often intrusive and sometimes fatal to the animal involved. For example, between 1963 and 1967, 35 grizzlies were tagged at McNeil River State Game Sanctuary. Eight bears died from the effects of the drugs and one drowned while it was tranquilized.

In one compilation of 13 bear studies in the Rocky Mountains of Canada and the United States, 7 of 90 known grizzly deaths were the result of the research itself. As tragic as this is, it is the

Radio-tracking has allowed biologists to follow grizzlies throughout the year. (Robert H. Busch)

price that wildlife pays when humans interfere, even with good intentions.

Many biologists have also had close calls themselves. In 1984, David Horning, an assistant of Bruce McLellan in the Canadian Border Grizzly Project, had a close encounter of the worst kind. Horning was checking a snare that held a yearling grizzly at the edge of a clearcut when the bear's mother appeared out of the brush. "Her legs were churning, and the brush was breaking," he recalls. "She was about 20 yards (18 meters) away and coming straight at me" (quoted in Turbak, 1984). Horning shot over the bear's head, then turned and ran across the clearcut. When he realized he could not outrun the bear, he turned to meet his attacker. But she was gone—it had been a bluff attack.

Ten years later, in 1994, researcher John Paczkowski was tracking a grizzly with a fixed-wing airplane in southern Alberta when the plane lost power and crash-landed on a road. Paczkowski was not injured in the crash, but he got a shock when he saw the bear he had been tracking walking down the road toward him. Paczkowski climbed the nearest tree and spent an uncomfortable night there until help arrived.

Despite the massive danger involved in working with grizzlies, a huge database of information has now been gathered that has provided crucial information on the great bear that can be used to manage it more effectively. Some of the more notable studies include the six studies described briefly below (see also the Bibliography).

Craighead Yellowstone Study

The earliest grizzly studies of note were those of John and Frank Craighead on the grizzlies of Yellowstone National Park.

In 1959, the two brothers examined more than 600 bears, taking basic measurements of length, weight, girth, and other physical data. The first grizzly ever to be tracked by radio transmitter was the famed bear Marian (Bear #40), collared and tagged by the Craigheads in 1961. Between 1961 and 1969, they radio-tracked 48 grizzlies and gained fame far and wide as a result of a television special by *National Geographic* that covered the brothers' research.

In 1971, however, the Craigheads spoke out against the sudden closing of the Yellowstone garbage dumps and warned of the negative effects this would have on the grizzlies. As a result, the brothers were no longer welcome to do research in the park, and the first major grizzly study on the continent came to a close.

Border Grizzly Project

From 1974 to 1984, the Director of the Border Grizzly Project (BGP) was biologist Charles Jonkel, who cut his bear teeth on black bear studies in Montana and polar bear work in the Canadian Arctic for the Canadian Wildlife Service.

This joint United States-Canada project performed studies on grizzly habitat, human impacts on the grizzly's environment, and on human-bear interactions. Its project area was a wide swath of northern Montana, Idaho, and Washington, spilling over into the southern edge of British Columbia.

The BGP did particularly interesting work in grizzly aversion at a lab in Missoula, Montana. There, biologists conducted experiments peppering nuisance bears housed in 7-foot by 10-foot (2-m by 3-m) concrete-block cells with various types of sprays, rubber bullets, and loud noises in order to study their responses and condition the bears to avoid humans and human activities. Of over 50 black bears and 6 grizzlies so treated, only 2 black bears and 1 grizzly caused further problems.

A Canadian counterpart of the BGP took root in 1978, headed by biologist Bruce McLellan, who studied grizzlies in the Flathead Valley of southern British Columbia. McLellan concentrated on habitat use and the effects of humans on the valley's beleagured bears.

Interagency Grizzly Bear Committee

In 1983, the National Park Service, U.S. Fish and Wildlife Service, Bureau of Land Management, and U.S. Forest Service joined forces to perform grizzly research under the name of the Interagency Grizzly Bear Committee. The next year, representatives of the Idaho Fish and Game Department; the Montana Department of Fish, Wildlife, and Parks; and the Wyoming Game and Fish Department joined the team. Members of the B.C. Wildlife Branch and Alberta Fish and Game Division joined later.

The Committee is based in Bozeman, Montana, and continues to coordinate grizzly research today, with a particular emphasis on the long-term management of grizzlies in the Greater Yellowstone Ecosystem.

Special emphasis has been placed on research on grizzly food habits and habitat use. The Committee has actively promoted closures of roads and clean-ups of garbage dumps in West Yellowstone and Cooke City, all with beneficial effects on grizzlies.

Another concrete result of the Committee's work is the publication of the 540-page *Grizzly Bear Compendium,* a volume of information on the natural history of the grizzly with a thick section of bibliographical references.

Eastern Slopes Grizzly Project

The purpose of this ongoing project is to study the effects of human development and activities on grizzly populations along the eastern slopes of the Canadian Rockies. The project is centered on the town of Canmore, Alberta, and includes much of Banff National Park and the 4,615-square mile (11,400-square km) Bow River drainage.

177

Wildlife overpasses near Banff, Alberta, have for some reason not been used by female grizzlies. (Courtesy H. Dempsey, Parks Canada)

The study began in 1993 and is manned by 24 University of Calgary students and staff, including grizzly bear expert Stephen Herrero and biologist Charles Mamo. Additional work under the project's auspices is performed by Dave Poll, a biologist with Parks Canada, ex-Parks Canada biologist Mike Gibeau, and John Kansas, a consulting biologist.

The project has an estimated budget of $1.5 million, donated by such diverse sponsors as Husky Oil and the Alberta Cattle Commission. The study has found that bears in the study area have a low population density and a relatively large home range.

One interesting finding of the Eastern Slopes Grizzly Project to date is that female grizzlies, for some reason, will not cross the Trans-Canada Highway or its animal overpasses or underpasses. Of 15 female grizzlies intensively studied over five years, not one has ever crossed the highway.

The overpasses, built at a staggering cost of almost $2 million each, are supposed to provide a safe route for animals across the busy stretch of highway between Banff and Lake Louise, where thousands of animals die each year. From 1981 to 1999, over 1,720 large animals including 28 bears, were killed on the highway and the adjacent Canadian Pacific Railway. Grizzly researcher Mike Gibeau (quoted in Remington, 2000) has called the stretch of highway "a Berlin Wall for wildlife."

Western Slopes Grizzly Project

The Western Slopes project is a sister study to the Eastern Slopes Grizzly Project. It is led by biologist John Woods, based in Glacier National Park, and veteran bear biologist Bruce McLellan of nearby Revelstoke. The study is centered on Golden, British Columbia, and includes much of Glacier and Yoho National Parks.

Foothills Model Forest Grizzly Bear Project

This new study, which began in April 1999, is aimed at determining the effects of human developments and activities on grizzly populations in Jasper National Park and along its eastern boundary. The $10 million study has already radio-collared 20 grizzlies so far and is using satellites to track bears six times a day, for 9 to 10 months a year. The project is also doing DNA work to determine the genetic relationships among the bears within the study area.

Despite the wealth of data that has come out of these and other research projects, much more information is required. When biologist Vivian Banci wrote the 1991 *Updated Status Report on the Grizzly Bear in Canada* for The Committee on the Status of Endangered Wildlife in Canada, she identified three particular research needs: population inventory, habitat inventory, and a means of linking the two. She also listed needs for research on grizzly bear biology and behavior, physiology, the impacts of research itself, and social value.

TRANSLOCATION

One measure of the grizzly's social value is the management technique called *translocation,* which is the capturing and moving of a problem bear to a new area. Although the public prefers translocation to the killing of a bear, the technique is not without its problems.

Firstly, translocating an animal as large as a grizzly is costly. The total costs of capturing, tranquilizing, and moving a bear can easily add up to over $1,000. If helicopter time is involved, the costs soar. For example, between 1989 and 1993, the B.C. Wildlife Branch translocated an average of 21 grizzlies per year. The average cost of each translocation was a steep $1,800.

Translocated bears such as this old male often find their way back home, wasting thousands of dollars in transportation costs. (Robert H. Busch)

Unfortunately, many translocated bears are killed by resident bears when the newcomer is dropped into their territory. In a 1982 study in Alaska by biologists S. D. Miller and W. B. Ballard, subadults and females with young were found to have the poorest rates of survival of all translocated grizzlies.

Another problem is that the translocated bear does not give up its bad habits but merely takes them elsewhere, so translocation sometimes merely amounts to moving a problem to another place. And translocated bears often find their way back home: In 12 studies of translocated black bears in Banff National Park, the rate of return was 60 to 70 percent.

Some bears even return over vast distances. One female grizzly in the southwest Yukon was moved 171 miles (113 km), a distance biologists thought was more than sufficient. In less than three days, she was back at the original capture site.

Translocated bears are often subadults, bears with little experience at life and a propensity for getting into trouble. Of 68 problem bears translocated by the Alberta Fish and Wildlife Division between 1974 and 1987, the greatest proportion (74 percent) were subadults. Thirty-two of the 68 bears were males. Most were translocated between July and September. The largest distance a bear was moved was 284 miles (430 km).

In many areas, there is a common pattern in the timing of grizzly bear complaints. Complaints often begin in April, just after bears emerge from dens. They rise until June, as bears forage for food, and then often peak in September, when bears are desperately attempting to put on the pounds prior to hibernation. October and November are usually quiet months, and complaints from December through March are very rare.

The persistence of a bear trying to return home is shown by a Montana grizzly in 1991. In April, the bear chased calves on a ranch near Kiowa on the Blackfoot Indian Reservation. Biologists trapped it and determined that the bear was a 400-pound (182-kg) male. They flew the bear 30 miles (45 km) into the Bob Marshall Wilderness and then released it. Two months later, it returned and killed some sheep. It was moved again, returned again, and killed a cow. Frustrated biologists moved it one last time, using firecrackers to scare it away from livestock. In July 1992, the grizzly returned once more and killed a cow on private land. Authorities finally gave up and shot it.

Shooting a bear is always a last resort, and many jurisdictions have set up strict guidelines for handling problem bears. In Alberta, for example, the bear control guidelines are as follows:

Type of Bear	1st Offense	2nd Offense	3rd Offense
older cub	move	move	take to zoo
subadult	move	move	shoot
sow	move	move	shoot
adult male	move	move	shoot

In addition to these guidelines, orphaned cubs in Alberta are taken to zoos. Old bears in poor physical condition are shot.

In general, older bears return home more often than younger bears. Males return more often than females. And the greater the distance the bear is moved (at greater cost), the better the chance the move will be successful.

Because of all the problems associated with translocations, many biologists suggest that funds instead be allocated to preventing the problems that caused the nuisance bear in the first place, prevention being cheaper than the cure.

AVERSIVE CONDITIONING

Aversive conditioning is a prevention techinique that involves giving a nuisance bear a painful or stressful experience in order to change its behavior. Nuisance bears are bears that have come into conflict with humans in some way, particularly by dining at garbage dumps.

The technique is far from new. In the early 1900s, C. J. Jones, a superintendent in Yellowstone National Park, lassoed a problem bear on its hind leg, strung the bear up from a tree limb, and gave it a good thrashing with a thin pole. It is not known if this unfortunate bear "learned its lesson" or continued to cause problems.

Today, bears have been bombarded with rubber bullets, loud noise, opened umbrellas, electric shocks, and even rock music in attempts to prevent negative behavior. To keep bears from eating domestic carrion, emetics or foul-tasting liquids can be poured over the food, in hopes that the bear will forever associate the bad taste or effect with that food source.

Biologist Charles Jonkel, who performed many aversive tests on grizzlies in Montana for the Border Grizzly Project, says that he has tried many methods, including "a bear 'thumper,' ultrasonic noise, shark repellent, rapidly inflating balloons and a spray of red pepper oil . . . The pepper spray has been most effective" (quoted in Domico, 1988).

The success of aversive conditioning depends on many factors, including the bear's age, number of experiences, severity of the conditioning, and availability of other sources of food. The conditioning is most successful with young bears that make one error and then receive aversive conditioning.

Aversive conditioning on young bears in the wild is done at both Katmai National Park and Preserve and Denali National Park and Preserve in Alaska. At Katmai, any young bear that wanders too close to camp is shot with rubber bullets that bounce harmlessly off the bear's thick rump.

At Denali, the bear is usually tranquilized and radio-collared. It is then moved to the backcountry and at intervals through the year is purposely tracked down. An artificial camp is set up, and if the bear approaches, it is shot with a harmless plastic slug that delivers a good sting. Technician John Dalle-Molle (quoted in Domico, 1988) says that "None of the bears we have hit with the slugs have appeared aggressive afterwards."

The biggest problem comes with older bears that are already food-conditioned. Poor physical condition may also be an obstacle to successful aversive conditioning.

Unfortunately, such conditioning is expensive and time-consuming. And as the Grizzly Bear Scientific Committee that advises the B.C. Wildlife Branch noted in 1995, "there is a strong movement within COs [conservation officers] to shoot all bears near communities." In other words, in the view of many conservation officers, shooting first and asking questions later is cheaper and easier.

PUBLIC EDUCATION

It is vital that the results of grizzly research reach the general public. The public must also be taught that proper garbage-disposal methods are a must in grizzly country. Hunters must be taught how to act in backcountry areas, how to keep clean camps, how to dispose of gut piles, how to distinguish male grizzlies from females, and even grizzly bears from black bears. And attitudes that result in illegal kills of grizzlies must be changed through a pervasive education and public awareness program.

Captive bears, like these two at Alberta's Calgary Zoo, are popular attractions to humans who see few glimpses of the wild in a high-tech world. (Robert H. Busch)

183

In 1973, a survey of tourists in Glacier National Park found that of 312 people surveyed, 65 percent had positive feelings toward the grizzly. And yet, the majority of grizzly-related complaints received by the Alberta Fish and Wildlife Division since 1980 have been merely of sightings of grizzlies in close proximity to areas used by humans.

Alberta bear biologist Rob Wielgus would like to see more education on the benign nature of grizzlies. "I've talked to people who are so afraid of grizzly bears that they don't want to go hiking," he says. "Or when they do go hiking, they have this constant fear that they might bump into a bear . . . this unreasonable fear . . . doesn't help human beings and it doesn't help the bears" (Hummel, 1991).

Another biologist, Tony Hamilton, has documented just how badly people tend to blow out of proportion innocent encounters with grizzlies. "A single incident gets translated beyond recognition each time it gets repeated," he says. "A story about one of our collared bears merely approaching someone eventually gets translated into an aggressive bear, or even a bear attack, when no such aggression was expressed at all" (Hamilton, in "Grizzlies studied," 1993).

Biologist Bruce McLellan (quoted in Turbak, 1998) is adamant that human intolerance is one of the biggest hurdles that grizzly conservationists have to face. He says, "The problem is not that grizzlies can't adapt to people, but that people can't adapt to grizzlies."

One instance of such intolerance occurred in 1984, when Montana rancher Keith Cable shot and killed a female grizzly and her cub when they strolled into his Mission Valley ranch yard. Another cub escaped and likely starved to death. "I damn well don't want them anywhere near my livestock or my family," said Cable (quoted in Turbak, 1984). "I may not know as much about them as some of the university people, but I know one thing: if a grizzly shows up in my corral, I'm going to kill the SOB."

The only hope of ever erasing such negative attitudes and the lack of tolerance toward grizzlies is through education.

LEGAL STATUS

The grizzly was classed as a threatened species in the lower 48 states under the Endangered Species Act on September 1, 1975. The illegal killing of a grizzly protected by the Act can result in fines of up to $20,000 and five years in prison.

The grizzly is listed as an endangered species in the lower 48 states and as a vulnerable species in Canada. (Robert H. Busch)

In 1982, the U.S. Fish and Wildlife Service approved a Grizzly Bear Recovery Plan, whose original objectives were the following:

1. Identify grizzly bear population goals that represent species recovery in measurable and quantifiable terms for the several regions that were determined to have suitable habitat for such populations, and to provide a data base that will allow informed decisions.
2. Identify population and habitat-limiting factors that account for the current populations existing at levels requiring threatened status under the Endangered Species Act.
3. Identify specific management measures needed to remove population limiting factors that will allow the populations to increase or sustain themselves at levels identified in the recovery goals.
4. Establish recovery of at least three grizzly bear populations in three distinct grizzly bear ecosystems in order to delist the species in the conterminous 48 states.

In the 1991 revised plan, the stated objective was "to reach viable populations of grizzly bears in each of the areas where grizzly bears are present or were suspected in 1975 in the states of Montana, Washington, Idaho, Wyoming, and Colorado where the habitat is able to support a viable population." The plan was revised again in October 1993, omitting Colorado altogether. At that time, it was estimated that only about 30 breeding female grizzlies remained in the Greater Yellowstone Ecosystem.

By early 1999, however, the great bear had made a good recovery in the Yellowstone National Park area. "Numbers appear to be on the rise, at least in the Greater Yellowstone Ecosystem," says grizzly bear recovery coordinator Chris Servheen (quoted in Chadwick, 1999). "Our counts indicate an absolute minimum of 262 grizzlies there and possible as many as 500. We intend to start delisting that population within a year."

By early 1999, it was estimated that 90 to 100 breeding female grizzlies lived within the Greater Yellowstone Ecosystem. Thirty-three females with 63 cubs of the year were counted in 1999. Since 1996, over 200 cubs are known to have been born in the Greater Yellowstone Ecosystem, giving real hope for the future.

Moves to preserve wilderness habitat since the 1960s have helped the grizzly rebound in many areas. (Robert H. Busch)

The U.S. Fish and Wildlife Service also intends to decide shortly whether or not to reintroduce grizzlies to the Selway-Bitterroot ecosystem, a small pocket of wilderness that sits west of Missoula along the Idaho border. The area consists of the 1.2 million acres (0.4 million hectares) of the Selway-Bitterroot Wilderness and adjoining 2.3 million-acre (0.9 million-hectare) Frank Church River of No Return Wilderness. Around this wilderness area would be a large tract of national forest and private lands that would not be deemed critical habitat for the grizzly.

The area where reintroduction has been proposed is not known to contain grizzlies today. In fact, there has been no photo, track, or other evidence of grizzly presence in that area since 1946. However, it is estimated that, properly managed, between 200 and 300 grizzlies could potentially survive if reintroduced into this remote wilderness.

Under a controversial 1985 provision of the Endangered Species Act, the bears would be designated as an "experimental, nonessential" population. This means that the bears would not have all the legal protection given in a normal species recovery plan.

A Citizens' Management Committee would be given the difficult task of balancing the bear's needs with those of loggers, ranchers, and recreational users who share the same lands. Committee members would be nominated by the governors of Idaho and Montana, and would work with state and federal wildlife agencies.

Unfortunately, the usual paranoia that follows grizzlies wherever they go, like an ugly shadow, has affected the Selway-Bitterroot reintroduction program. As soon as the plans were announced, there was a howl of protest from some local residents. One citizen wrote to the local paper, "As soon as they move more grizzlies in here, that's the last time I'm ever going into the woods."

The draft Environmental Impact Statement by the U.S. Fish and Wildlife Service identifies this proposal as the "preferred alternative" for grizzly restoration in the Selway-Bitterroot Ecocsystem. If the proposal is passed, 4 to 6 bears per year would be reintroduced to the area for up to five years. All would be radio-collared for easier tracking. The ultimate goal is a grizzly population of more than 300 bears within 50 to 75 years, which would make this the third-largest grizzly population in the lower 48 states. The proposal is backed by the National Wildlife Federation, which inititated the restoration proposal back in 1994. It is opposed by both the Idaho Congressional delegation and Idaho Governor Dick Kemp Thorne. If approved, reintroduction may begin as soon as 2002.

In 1999, the Committee on the Status of Wildlife in Canada (COSEWIC) listed the Canadian plains grizzlies as extirpated, meaning "no longer existing in the wild in Canada, but occurring elsewhere." All other Canadian grizzly populations are classed as "vulnerable," meaning the bear is "a species of special concern because of characteristics that make it particularly sensitive to human activities or natural events." There is no national recovery plan for the grizzly in Canada, because its grizzly population is fairly large and stable.

Internationally, the grizzly is protected from trade under the Convention on International Trade in Endangered Species of Wild Fauna and Flora (CITES). CITES represents an international agreement first signed in 1973. Its purpose is to restrict and regulate international trade in endangered species, their parts, and any products made from those parts.

The grizzly is listed as an Appendix II species in the CITES agreement. This means that it is not yet deemed endangered, but may become so if trade is not regulated. Any species traded must have an export permit issued by the government of the exporting country before export is allowed.

The B.C. Grizzly Bear Conservation Strategy

Because almost half of the grizzlies in Canada live in British Columbia, that province's grizzly management practices are crucial to the future of the Canadian grizzly.

In June 1995, the B.C. Wildlife Branch finally announced a new conservation strategy for grizzlies, stating that "unless steps are taken now to conserve grizzly bear populations in British Columbia, this animal could disappear from our landscape forever."

In a 70-page report, the Wildlife Branch recognized the effect that British Columbia's booming human population growth, the fastest in Canada, will have on grizzlies. The provincial population is expected to double by the year 2065, and, as former B.C. Wildlife Branch director Ray Halliday admitted, "more people means fewer bears."

The strategy concedes that forestry practices in British Columbia have not historically been compatible with the feeding and denning

A **Future** for the **Grizzly**

GRIZZLY BEAR
Conservation Strategy for British Columbia
Province of British Columbia
Ministry of Environment, Lands and Parks

The Grizzly Bear Conservation Strategy is a sound plan for the management of almost half the grizzlies in Canada. (Robert H. Busch)

needs of the grizzlies; after actual habitat loss, it predicts that over the next 5 years, forestry will be the highest negative factor on grizzly ecosystems throughout the province. However, it expresses hope that the new Forest Practises Code will force loggers to change their ways. It states that a new Forest Practises Code field guide for grizzlies will "ensure that . . . logging . . . outside of protected areas does not adversely affect key grizzly bear habitat."

The strategy recommends a system of protected areas, travel corridors, and no-hunting zones to preserve critical grizzly habitat. Suggested protected areas include the lower Stikine River, Kechika-Muskwa, Southern Selkirk Mountains, and Kingcome Inlet areas. The first two of these have historically suffered from bear poaching.

The strategy's ultimate objective "is to have one large core for each of the province's grizzly bear ecosystems and to ensure that these are linked with sufficient habitats to support grizzly bear populations." Unfortunately, the strategy states that the establishment of Grizzly Bear Management Areas "will not necessarily prohibit resource extraction," meaning that once again logging and the preservation of bear habitat will come into conflict.

The strategy recommends additional research into grizzly bear habitats and populations within the province, recognizing the need for hard data. The research is partly financed by a small surcharge to grizzly hunting licenses. The surcharge is expected to raise about $160,000 per year for grizzly conservation efforts.

Also planned are educational efforts aimed at children, hunters, and hikers. The strategy recommends closer and better regulation of garbage dumps, with a $250,000 budget earmarked for improved waste control. It also proposes increased enforcement and stiffer fines for poachers, with a minimum $1,000 fine for a first offense and a maximum fine of $25,000.

One concrete result of the strategy has been the formation of a Scientific Committee that advises the B.C. Wildlife Branch on biological aspects of bear management. The Committee includes some of the top names in bear biology on the continent, including Canadian scientists Stephen Herrero, Tony Hamilton, Bruce McLellan, Paul Paquet, Wayne McCrory, and Rob Wielgus, as well as American expert Chris Servheen.

The Committee has made a long list of "hot spots" within British Columbia where the great bear is already in big trouble, including the Northern Cascades, Cabinet-Yaak, Pemberton, Granby Kettle, Selkirks, Jumbo, Babine, Elk Valley, and Cassiar areas. Grizzlies in the southern half of the province are described as suffering from particularly severe population declines.

A Conflict Management Committee has been formed to advise on the development of improved waste disposal sites and 17 sites have had electric fences installed, including those at Kitimat, Stewart, Revelstoke, Elkford, and Mackenzie.

The B.C. Wildife Branch has won praise for closing grizzly hunting in the Okanagan and southern Selkirk Mountains in 1995. In 1993, friends of the grizzly were furious when 14 grizzly hunting permits were allocated near Kokanee Glacier in the southern Selkirk Mountians. Bear biologists Wayne McCrory and Erica Mallum had determined in a 1992 study that the area had almost four times the recommended grizzly harvest figure of 4 percent. They concluded that an immediate closure to grizzly hunting in the area was necessary for the bear population to recover, but their report was ignored.

In fact, many times in the past, the B.C. Wildlife Branch has come under heavy fire for putting dollars first and bears last. For example, in 1990, the 20 to 30 grizzlies left in the Granby Park area of southern British Columbia were the first Canadian grizzlies to be nationally identified as threatened. Conservationists were therefore outraged when the B.C. government approved 18 logging cutblocks in the Goatskin Special Resource Management Zone near Granby Park in 1996.

However, public outcry has softened the attitudes of many government wildlife agencies, including the B.C. Wildlife Branch. In February 2000, the failure of salmon runs along the northwest British Columbia coast hit bear populations hard. After 6 starved grizzlies ventured into the tiny community of Rivers Inlet and were shot by conservation officers, the B.C. Wildlife Branch was quick to close the spring grizzly hunt in the area. Conservationists were pleased with the move, hoping that it was evidence of a new direction in grizzly management.

They are disappointed, however, that the Grizzly Bear Conservation Strategy has not made more concrete progress. Nearly five years after it was announced with great fanfare by the provincial government, no new protected areas or travel corridors have been established, no additional conservation officers have been hired by the B.C. Wildlife Branch, and the promised Forest Practises Code field guide for grizzlies has yet to be written.

Conservationists are concerned that much of the conservation strategy consists merely of recommendations, which may or may not be followed.

Critics also note that British Columbia is horribly understaffed when it comes to conservation officers, with only 136 field officers available to patrol the entire province. Each officer patrols an average territory of over 3,000 square miles (7,770 square km), an impossibly large area. According to the Raincoast Conservation Society, during all of 1995, conservation officers were in the field for only three days in the entire central British Columbia coastal area. Conservationists doubt that enough money can be found to effectively increase the conservation department; in recent years the number of field staff has actually been decreasing.

Conservationists also state that there are well over a hundred rural garbage dumps in central and northern British Columbia plus hundreds of roadside garbage containers and recreation sites that do not have fencing of any sort or use bear-proof containers. Some of these dumps have chronic grizzly problems. The dump at Mackenzie, in north-central British Columbia, was an especially severe problem dump; 70 bears near the dump were either killed or relocated within a 1-year period prior to the dump's closure.

It is estimated that upgrading the northern rural dumps alone would cost well over half a million dollars. However, the conservation strategy has earmarked only half this figure for improved waste control throughout the entire province.

The plan has updated the provincial hunting regulations, now allowing the hunting of grizzlies only on a limited-entry basis. This is a strategy whereby grizzly hunters selected through a lottery system can hunt grizzlies only during a specified period, after paying a larger hunting fee. Many people question the use of such a system and whether it will result in fewer bears being killed.

The new fines proposed for poaching still seem low, as well. Jim Hart, the senior conservation officer in Fort Nelson, British Columbia (quoted in Pynn, 1995), describes the new fines as "pretty much irrelevant." In addition to stiffer fines, conservationists would like to see poachers receive jail sentences plus seizure of their arms, vehicles, boats, or any aircraft used in poaching activities.

Some conservation officers would like to see the sale of grizzly pelts banned altogether to save the big bear. Joe Caravetta, a conservation officer in the northern British Columbia community of Dease Lake (quoted in Pynn, 1995), says, "Some people shoot just to sell the hides, which is legal. That's got to be banned." In Canada, the grizzly's pelt is exceeded in value only by that of the polar bear. Both are listed as vulnerable species by the Committee on the Status of Endangered Species in Canada (COSEWIC).

Caravetta is also critical of the fact that native Indians throughout the province are exempt from limited-entry hunting regulations.

"There can't be two laws," he says (quoted in Pynn, 1995). Native Indians who are British Columbia residents do not have to obtain a hunting license of any kind nor take any hunter training program, which makes little sense in terms of both wildlife management and hunter safety.

However, native rights are a touchy political subject in Canada, and the government is loathe to add fuel to an already-blazing inferno.

GENETIC DIVERSITY

Recently, it has been discovered that the muskoxen of Banks Island in the high Arctic face a problematic future due to a loss of genetic diversity. The muskoxen, being isolated on an island, have become inbred, and all share the same basic genetic makeup.

Biologists have found that the genetic variation within the 47,000 muskoxen of Banks Island is a thousand times less than among herds

Grizzlies are the very essence of wilderness. (Adrian Dorst)

of mainland oxen. So similar is their genetic material that DNA samples of 7 of the animals are virtually identical.

Many grizzly populations living on ecological "islands" surrounded by human habitation are likely going to suffer from the same lack of genetic variation, if they are already not affected. If the 47,000 muskoxen of Banks Island have genetic problems, what must be the genetic situation with the 400 grizzlies in Yellowstone National Park?

Generally speaking, species that are dispersed over a wide area and have low densities, may have physical or behavioral adaptations unique to each subpopulation. Many of these unique traits may have a genetic basis. *Genetic variability,* therefore, is the variability in qualities such as height, weight, or resistance to disease within animals in a species as determined by genes. A population of animals with low genetic diversity could be decimated by an outbreak of a disease caused by a new virus, for example.

A related problem is *inbreeding,* the mating of closely related individuals. Inbreeding in mammals can cause blindness, loss of weight in juveniles, reproduced reproductive ability, and reduced lifespan. Matings between individuals that have limited genetic variability can result in direct mortality or reduced fertility in later generations.

Often, there is a typical inbreeding cycle beginning with abnormal sperm, which leads to infertility, which is also linked to a weakened immune system. A weak immune system leaves a species vulnerable to the perils of bacteria, viruses, and parasites. A relatively weak infection that would have minimal effects on one subpopulation could therefore have devastating effects on an inbred subpopulation.

So in the end, the future of the big bear may not just depend on how many bears there are, but on the diversity of their microscopic genetic makeup.

Today, that makeup can be studied through DNA analysis of blood, skin, fur, or tissue. Only in the last few years has DNA analysis entered the biologists' toolkit, however. Many DNA studies of grizzlies are currently underway, and many biologists are expecting the worst.

An influx of new genes is necessary to reduce the risk of inbreeding and loss of genetic variation. For isolated subpopulations, however, such as the grizzlies of Yellowstone National Park, the very isolation of the park makes such an influx difficult. Many other sub-populations of grizzlies, such as those in the Cabinet-Yaak or North Cascades, or on Alaska's Chichagof Island, are just as threatened.

The 1993 Grizzly Bear Recovery Plan for the United States recognized the problem of genetic diversity as applied to grizzly populations, stating: "It is widely accepted in conservation biology that island populations of any species are subject to high rates of extinction and that these rates are directly related to the size of the island."

This leads to one of the oldest debates in conservation biology—namely, whether a few large animal preserves are better than a number of smaller ones.

Some biologists believe that large areas are better for conserving a species, for they give that species more space in which to breed and live. If an area is too small, there is a great deal of risk that a catastrophe could wipe out the entire population. And it seems logical that the larger the population, the greater the chance of it surviving in the long term.

Others believe that instead of a few large preserves, there should be a number of smaller ones, to minimize the risk of a disaster decimating one subpopulation and to allow the migration of species from one preserve to another, to exchange genes and improve genetic diversity. Thus the choice—a few large preserves or a number of smaller ones.

Even if an area is very large, there is also a risk that the animals in that area may not have enough genetic diversity. The 2.2 million acres (0.9 million hectares) of Yellowstone National Park is impressive geographically, but may not be large enough to support sufficient genetic diversity in a grizzly population. Biologist Mark Schaffer calculated that a population of at least 50 Yellowstone grizzlies was necessary to ensure short-term survival of that population, but that at least 500 were necessary for continuing adaptation and long-term survival. Biologists call this latter figure the *minimum viable population,* or MVP. Unfortunately, Schaffer did not incorporate catastrophic events into his calculations, and thus likely underestimated the population sizes needed for survival.

In his 1978 PhD thesis, Schaffer estimated that for the isolated bears of Yellowstone National Park, a population of less than 30 to 70 bears, occupying less than 965 to 2,857 square miles (2,500 to 7,400 square km), had less than a 95-percent chance of surviving for 100 years. Others have calculated numbers that range from 40 to 125 bears. When inbreeding and catastrophic events are taken into account, these numbers are likely too low.

MVP analyses have been performed for other areas as well. Biologists Wayne McCrory and Stephen Herrero in 1987 attempted to estimate the MVP for bear populations in British Columbia. Assuming a best-case scenario that included a high reproductive rate and an adult female percentage of the population of over 50 percent, the two bear biologists came up with a MVP of 393 bears, a figure that is possible only for populations in the most remote northern corners of the province. If their figures are correct, the small populations of bears in southern British Columbia are doomed.

One of the best ways to improve genetic diversity is to introduce bears from other areas, a conservation move that has taken place in the Cabinet-Yaak area of Montana and Idaho and was once considered for the Yellowstone grizzly population.

These high-cost moves clearly demonstrate the ends to which mankind will go to save the great bear.

The Y2Y Project

One of the hopes for the grizzly's future across North America rests with an audacious project known as the Yellowstone to Yukon Conservation Initiative (Y2Y). The project envisages an 1,800-mile (2,727-km) spread of connected parks, wildlife movement corridors, and protected areas stretching from Yellowstone National Park to the Yukon. Peter Aengst (1999), Outreach Coordinator for the project, describes it as "a proactive, holistic vision for the long-term health of the Rocky Mountain region."

The project originated in a classic 1967 book by biologists Robert MacArthur and Edward O. Wilson, entitled *The Theory of Island Biogeography*. In the book, the two biologists discussed their findings that island plant and animal communities are more subject to extinction than non-island species, a simple concept that proved to have major consequences for wildlife conservation.

A few years after the book came out, biologist Michael Soulé extended the MacArthur-Wilson theory to land-based ecosystems. He stated that clearcuts, ranches, and urban developments are just as limiting to terrestrial species as the ocean is to island-based species. Soulé wondered if the isolated groups of animals living in

North America's parks and refuges could face the same high extinction rate as island species. His ideas were widely debated at the First International Conference on Conservation Biology in 1978.

Twelve years later, the World Wildlife Fund (Canada) released its Conservation Strategy for Large Carnivores in Canada. The Strategy noted that carnivores are often "keynote" species, whose health is a

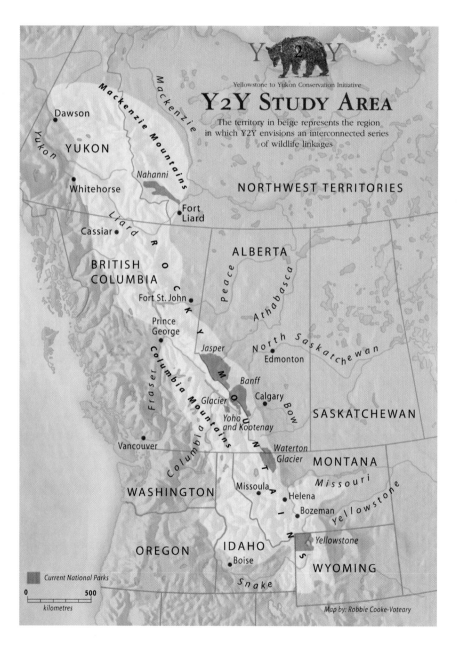

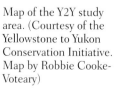

Map of the Y2Y study area. (Courtesy of the Yellowstone to Yukon Conservation Initiative. Map by Robbie Cooke-Voteary)

good measure of the general health of the rest of the ecosystem. The Strategy recommended the establishment of large Carnivore Conservation Areas, with the pointed comment that "we must also keep in mind the importance of linking them."

In 1991, Soulé met with Dave Foreman, cofounder of the radical conservation group Earth First! The meeting led to the establishment of The Wildlands Project, a group whose mission is to develop a conservation network of wilderness areas surrounded by buffer zones and linked by conservation corridors.

Two years later, Harvey Locke, an Alberta environmental lawyer, convened a meeting of Rocky Mountain conservation biologists who discussed designing a conservation network along the rocky spine of the continent, where the highest concentrations of North American carnivores still remain. Out of this meeting evolved the Y2Y initiative.

In October 1997, over 300 biologists, activists, and other interested parties gathered in Waterton National Park to ratify the Y2Y Project as a dream worth pursuing. As a campaign symbol for the initiative, the group chose the grizzly.

To be a success, the project must realize the cooperation of a long list of local, regional, provincial, federal, and territorial agencies on both sides of the Canada–United States border.

The dream is anchored by five major park systems: Yellowstone and Glacier National Parks in the United States and Banff, Jasper, and Waterton National Parks in Canada. Many of the gaps between existing parks are huge. The distance between the Yellowstone ecosystem in Montana and the Selway-Bitterroot system in Idaho, for example, is over 240 miles (363 km).

The Castle Wilderness gap north of Waterton National Park is almost as big. The closing of these gaps is crucial to the success of the Y2Y project; not one radio-tracked grizzly in the United States in the past 25 years has ever crossed from one ecosystem to another when the gap has been over 40 miles (61 km).

Critics also point out that about 2 million people live within the project area, and that number is expected to double over the next 30 years. There are also over 400,000 miles (606,000 km) of roads within the area already. Of 320 major watersheds in the area, only 28 remain roadless—for now.

One essential corridor is that between the Northern Continental Divide Ecosystem and the Mission Mountains of Montana, where a dozen or so grizzlies live in a small remote pocket of habitat.

To help ensure their survival, the U.S. Fish and Wildlife Service established a conservation plan in 1995 that limits development harmful to grizzlies on 33,000 private acres (12,741 hectares). Where another 83,000 acres (32,046 hectares) were held by a timber company, the Service called for the closing of logging roads, careful scheduling of logging to disturb the bears as little as possible, and preservation of riparian habitats. Similar Habitat Conservation Plans exist elsewhere, an excellent idea that Canada would do well to emulate.

Other recent moves that help push the Y2Y project along include the creation by the British Columbia government of the new Muskwa-Kechika Provincial Park and Protected Area in the northern part of that province, the creation by the Alberta government of the Bow Valley Wildland Park, the closing of the Banff National Park airstrip, and the signing of an agreement between the United States National Park Service and the Canadian Park Service naming the Y2Y project as a joint priority.

The project has not been without its detractors, however. Jack Munro, outspoken chairman of B.C.'s Forest Alliance (quoted in Finkel, 1999), says that "Y2Y would be devastating to the timber business. It'll destroy the industries that built this continent." Munro alleges that up to 80,000 jobs would be lost in British Columbia alone as a result of the Y2Y project, incorrectly assuming that the initiative would shut down all human activities throughout the area.

Some biologists fear that the complex of political jurisdictions involved will kill the dream before it begins. They point to the years of delay in the reintroduction of the wolf to Yellowstone National Park caused by petty squabbling between Montana state biologists and federal U.S. Fish and Wildlife Service representatives.

However, more positive critics point to that same project and to the lessons of cooperation it provided. As biologist Dian Fossey wrote in *Gorillas in the Mist,* "when you realize the value of all life, you dwell less on what is past and concentrate more on the preservation of the future."

GLOBAL WARMING

One pervasive threat to all living things is global warming. *Global warming* is loosely defined as the warming effect of carbon dioxide and other gases that are accumulating above the Earth and acting as an insulating blanket, keeping heat in and raising atmospheric temperatures. During the past 150 years, the amount of carbon dioxide in the atmosphere has increased by 25 percent, there has been a 100-percent increase in methane, and new heat-trapping chemicals such as the chlorofluorocarbons and halons have been emitted in great quantities through various human activities.

According to many scientists, atmospheric temperatures may rise by 1.8° to 5.4°F (1.5° to 4.5°C) over the next hundred years. At the end of the last Ice Age, the Earth similarly warmed up by about 9°F (5°C), but it did so over several thousand years. That same temperature rise in only a century is expected to have widespread effects on the animals and plants that live on planet Earth. Some are predicting the worst ecological disaster to hit humankind since the medieval plagues.

Global warming is expected to have the most severe effects in the middle and higher latitudes, where temperatures are expected to be 50 to 100 percent higher than the average for Earth as a whole.

George M. Woodwell, President and Director of the Woods Hole Research Centre in Massachusetts (quoted in Leggett, 1990), predicts that a general warming of 0.12° to 1.2°F (0.1° to 1.0°C) per decade would result in "the rapid destruction of forests without their replacement . . . Under such circumstances, forests are often replaced by savannah, shrubland, or grassland."

Dr. Woodwell also predicts that a 1.2°F (1°C) increase in temperature would extend the forest-grassland transition zones in the northern hemisphere about 60 to 100 miles (91 to 151 km) north. In the past, such temperature changes have resulted in the mass migration of vertebrates and the loss of species which could not either adapt or migrate.

And so what will be the effect of global warming upon the grizzly? Many biologists predict that as forests recede and move northward, the grizzly will follow, and its southern pockets of habitat will be vacated.

The grizzlies of Yellowstone National Park are in particular danger from global warming, because they are the southernmost grizzly population surviving today. If the world does warm up, two of the Yellowstone grizzlies' main foods may disappear. Whitebark pine cones, which grow only at elevations above 8,000 feet (2,439 m), may become extremely limited as their alpine habitat warms. Army cutworm moths, which prefer elevations above 10,000 feet (3,049 m), will likely disappear from the park altogether.

It is in the preservation of pristine wilderness that the future of the grizzly lies. (Robert H. Busch)

In many parts of Alberta and British Columbia, though, a move north would move the grizzly away from population centers, which tend to be focused in the southern halves of the provinces. As it moves into less-populated areas, the grizzly's population may actually increase in these areas.

The picture is not quite so rosy for the Kodiak bears, however. These giants, being isolated on an island chain, may move higher and higher up into the mountains as the lower forests are replaced by grass or shrubland. Ultimately, as their habitat diminishes, and the bears are unable to move north because of the surrounding ocean, the subspecies will begin to die out and may disappear altogether.

Or will it? Some biologists think that the great bear's ability to eat a wide variety of foods and live in a wide variety of habitats will cushion it somewhat from the effects of global warming. Only time will tell.

CONCLUSION

When I was a child many years ago, I used to enjoy Sunday trips to the town of Banff, Alberta, because of the wealth of wildlife we would always see by the side of the road. Elk, deer, moose, bighorn sheep, and even bears could almost always be counted upon to make an appearance. But no more: The boom of human activities in the area has pushed the animals back into the furthest reaches of Banff National Park. On my last trip along that same stretch of highway we used to travel just 30 years ago, the largest animal I saw was a squirrel.

Multiplied many times over across the whole continent, it is the same old story. The lush pristine habitat that once was is now gone or altered in such a way that it is no longer a safe haven for wildlife. And for many species slated for reintroduction, often there is simply no home to return to.

The checkerboard of destruction caused by clearcut logging simply must stop, for it has decimated species from mice to moose. But the political power of large logging companies is awesome. Unfortunately, animals have neither wallets nor votes. As Pat Conroy wrote in *The Prince of Tides,* "Whenever Big Money goes up against the Environment, Big Money always wins. It's an American law."

I find it especially disturbing that there are a few people who do not see the wisdom of preserving habitat, and indeed see it as a threat to

A grizzly fishing at twilight. (Robert McCaw)

their personal freedom. Recently, Peg Warner, spokesperson for Montanans For Multiple Use, stated that "Lots of roads are closed because of grizzlies, and this essentially locks the public out of their own forests" (quoted in Turbak, 1993). Despite the names of these so-called "wise-use" groups, their aims are all too often both narrow and selfish.

Part of the biological reason for conserving the grizzly is that it is a "keystone" species, one whose survival influences the survival of other species who share the same habitat. It is no accident that where you find grizzlies, you also find cougars, wolverines, mountain caribou, and a host of other threatened or rare species.

The wild spaces inhabited by the remaining grizzlies also support a wide spectrum of endangered plant species. In Montana, 40 percent of the state's vascular plants of special concern live within grizzly habitat. By saving that habitat, we save not only the grizzly, but everything from lichens to lynx.

Much of the grizzly's appeal is not biological, but spiritual. Grizzlies are the sheer essence of wilderness; to lose any more bears would truly be a crime against nature and against those of us who need and love the wild. In 1984, Montana author Gary Turbak quoted grizzly biologist Bruce McLellan in an article for *Equinox*: McLellan spoke passionately about the interconnection between grizzlies and wilderness, saying, "I've hiked around Colorado, where there are no grizzlies, and it's sterile. The land is just not wild. Sure, a mauling is terrible, but the potential for a mauling is wonderful." It is what makes the wild truly wild.

It is in the preservation of wilderness habitat that the future of the grizzly and all of the other great predators relies. As bear biologist Charles Jonkel (quoted in Turbak, 1984) says, "The grizzly is a good barometer for measuring how we're treating the environment. If we've got grizzly bears, then we're probably taking good care of the land . . . if we protect the habitat, the grizzlies will be there."

And so ultimately, the choice is up to us: Do we humans wish to share this planet with the myriad of other species that now exist? Or do we wish to control the planet, exterminating all species except for the greatest predator of all—humankind?

To me, destroying habitat so that we push the grizzly back further and further into remote mountain refuges and parks is like rolling back a beautiful carpet to reveal a bare ugly floor beneath. Both actions diminish aesthetics that we hold dear. And both leave the world a little uglier and emptier for us all.

APPENDIX I

Bear Conservation Organizations

Brown Bear Resources, 222 North Higgins, Missoula, MT 59802

Craighead Environmental Research Institute, 201 South Wallace Avenue, Ste. B20, Bozeman, MT 59715

Craighead Wildlife-Wildlands Institute, 5200 Upper Miller Creek Road, Missoula, MT 59803

Denali Foundation Grizzly Fund, Box 212, Denali Park, AK 99755

Great Bear Foundation, P.O. Box 9383, Missoula, MT 59807

Greater Yellowstone Coalition, P.O. Box 1874, Bozeman, MT 59715

Grizzly Discovery Center, P.O. Box 996, West Yellowstone, MT 59758

Grizzly Project, P.O. Box 957, Nelson, BC, Canada V1L 6A5

International Association for Bear Research and Management, 2841 Forest Avenue, Berkeley, CA 94705

North American Bear Centre, P.O. Box 161, Ely, MN 55731

North American Bear Society, P.O. Box 55774, Phoenix, AZ 85078

Predator Defense Institute, P.O. Box 5079, Eugene, OR 97405

Valhalla Wilderness Society, P.O. Box 329, New Denver, BC, Canada V0K 1S0

Yellowstone Grizzly Foundation, 581 Expedition Drive, Evanston, WY 82930

Formerly Recognized Grizzly Bear Species of North America

Ursus	*absarokus*	Absaroka grizzly
	alexandrae	Alexander grizzly
	andersoni	Anderson's bear
	apache	Apache grizzly
	arizonae	Arizona grizzly
	atnarko	Atnarko grizzly
	ausorgus	(common name unknown)
	bairdi	Baird grizzly
	californicus	California coastal grizzly
	caurinus	Lynn Canal grizzly
	chelan	Chelan grizzly
	chelidonias	Jervis Inlet grizzly
	colusus	Sacramento Valley grizzly
	crassodon	Big-tooth grizzly
	crassus	Thickset grizzly

cressonus	Chitna bear
dalli	Dall brown bear
dusorgus	(common name unknown)
eltonclarki	Sitka grizzly
eulophus	Admiralty crested bear
eximius	Knik bear
henshawi	Henshaw grizzly
hoots	Stikine brown bear
horriaeus	New Mexico grizzly
horriaeus texensis	Texas grizzly
horribilis alascensis	Alaska grizzly
idahoensis	Idaho grizzly
imperator	Yellowstone park big grizzly
innuitus	Inuit bear
inopinatus	Great yellow bear
insularis	Island grizzly
internationalis	Alaska boundary grizzly
kennerlyi	Sonora grizzly
kidderi kidderi	Kidder bear
kidderi tundrensis	Tundra bear
klamathensis	Klamath grizzly
kluane	Kluane grizzly
kluane impiger	Industrious grizzly
kwakiutl	Kwakiutl grizzly
kwakitul neglectus	Admiralty Island grizzly
kwakiutl warburtoni	Warburton Pike grizzly
macfarlani	MacFarlane bear
macrodon	Twin Lakes grizzly
magister	Southern California grizzly
mendocinensis	Mendocino grizzly
mirabilis	Strange grizzly

mirus	Yellowstone Park grizzly
navaho	Navaho grizzly
nelsoni	Nelson grizzly
nortoni	Yakutat grizzly
nuchek	Nuchek brown bear
ophrus	(common name unknown)
orgiloides	Alsek grizzly
orgilos	Glacier Bay grizzly
pallasi	Pallas grizzly
pellyensis	Pelly grizzly
perturbans	Mount Taylor grizzly
pervagor	Lilloet grizzly
phaeonyx	Tanana grizzly
phaeonyx latifrons	Broad-fronted grizzly
planiceps	Flat-headed grizzly
pulchellus ereunetes	Kootenay grizzly
pulchellus pulchellus	Upper Yukon grizzly
richardsoni	Barren ground grizzly
rogersi isonphagus	Black Hills Grizzly
rogersi rogersi	Rogers grizzly
rungiusi rungiusi	Rungius grizzly
rungiusi sagittalis	Crested grizzly
russelli	Pelly grizzly
selkirki	Forest grizzly
sheldoni	Montague Island grizzly
shirasi	Shiras brown bear
shoshone	Shoshone grizzly
shoshone canadensis	Canada grizzly
sitkensis	Sitka brown bear
stikeenensis	Stikine grizzly
tahltanicus	Tahltan grizzly

toklat	Toklat grizzly
townsendi	Townsend bear
tularensis	Tejon grizzly
utahensis	Utah grizzly
vetularctos inopinatus	Patriarchal bear
washake	Washakie grizzly

Bibliography

Aengst, Peter. "The Yellowstone to Yukon Initiative: Preserving the Heart of North America." *Banff National Park Research Updates,* 2(1):7 (Spring 1999).

Alaska Hunting Regulations. Juneau, AK: Alaska Fish and Game Department, 1999. 110 pp.

Andreef, Monica. "On grizzly patrol in the Rockies." *The Vancouver Sun,* p. A5 (Oct. 3, 1996).

Applegate, R. D., L. L. Rogers, D. A. Casteel, and J. M. Novak. "Germination of cow parsnip seeds from grizzly bear feces." *Journal of Mammalogy,* 60(3):655 (1979).

Ashworth, William. *Bears: Their Life and Behavior.* New York: Crown Publishers, Inc., 1992.

Atwell, G., D. L. Boone, J. Gustafson, and V. D. Berns. "Brown bear summer use of alpine habitat on the Kodiak National Wildlife Refuge." *International Conference on Bear Research and Management,* 4:297–305 (1980).

Ballard, W. B. "Brown bear kills gray wolf." *Canadian Field Naturalist,* 94(1):91 (1980).

Banci, Vivian. *The status of the grizzly bear in Canada in 1990.* Ottawa, ON: Committee on the Status of Endangered Wildlife in Canada, 1991. 171 pp.

Banfield, A. W. F. *The Mammals of Canada.* Toronto: University of Toronto Press, 1974.

Bass, Rick. "Grizzlies: Are They Out There?" *Audubon,* 95(5):66–79 (Sept.–Oct. 1993).

British Columbia Ministry of Environment, Lands and Parks Hunting & Trapping Regulations Synopsis 1999–2000. Victoria, BC: Ministry of Environment, Lands, and Parks, 1999. 98 pp.

Brown, David E. and John A. Murray, comp. *The Last Grizzly and Other Southwestern Bear Stories.* Tucson, AZ: University of Arizona Press, 1988.

Brown, Gary. *The Great Bear Almanac.* New York: Lyons & Burford, 1993.

Burland, Cottie. *North American Indian Mythology.* Middlesex, England: Newnes Books, 1965.

Busch, Robert H. *Valley of the Grizzlies.* Toronto: Stoddart Publishing Company Ltd., 1998.

Byers, C. Randall and George A. Bettas. *Boone and Crockett Club Records of North American Big Game.* Missoula, MT: Boone and Crockett Club, 1999.

Carey, Alan. *In the Path of the Grizzly.* Flagstaff, AZ: Northland Publishing, 1986.

Carr, H. D. "Distribution, numbers and mortality of grizzly bears in and around Kananaskis Country, Alberta." Edmonton, AB: Department of Forestry, Lands and Wildlife, Research Series No. 3, 1989.

Chadwick, Douglas. "Grizz: Of men and the great bear." *National Geographic,* 169(2):182–213 (Feb. 1986).

————. "Helping a Great Bear Hang On." *National Wildlife,* 37(1):22–31 (Dec. 1998/Jan. 1999).

Conroy, Pat. *The Prince of Tides.* New York: Houghton Mifflin Co., 1986.

Conservation of Grizzly Bears in British Columbia: Background Report. Victoria, BC: Ministry of Environment, Lands and Parks, May 1995. 70 pp.

Craighead, Frank C. *Track of the Grizzly.* San Francisco: Sierra Club Books, 1979.

Craighead, John J. and J. A. Mitchell. "Grizzly bear (*Ursus arctos*)." *In* J. A. Chapman and G. A. Feldhamer (eds.). *Wild mammals of North America: Biology, Management, Economics.* Baltimore, MD: John Hopkins Press, 1982.

Cunningham, Dave. "The Bear Facts." *British Columbia Report,* 3(42):20–22 (June 22, 1992).

Day, Beth. *Grizzlies in Their Backyard.* Surrey, BC: Heritage House Publishing Co. Ltd., 1994.

Dobie, J. Frank. *The Ben Lilly Legend.* Austin, TX: University of Texas Press, 1982 (reprint).

Domico, Terry. *Bears of the World.* New York: Facts on File, 1988.

Dood, A. R., R. D. Brannon, and R. D. Mace. *Final programmatic environmental impact statement: The grizzly bear in northwestern Montana.* Helena, MT: Montana Department of Fish, Wildlife and Parks, 1986. 287 pp.

Egbert, Allen L. and Michael H. Luque. "Among Alaska's Brown Bears." *National Geographic,* 148(3):428–442 (Sept. 1975).

Ewers, John C. *The Blackfeet: Raiders on the Northwest Plains.* Norman, OK: University of Oklahoma Press, 1958.

Ewing, Susan. *The Great Rocky Mountain Nature Factbook.* Portland, OR: Westwinds Press, 1999.

Finkel, Michael. "From Yellowstone to Yukon." *Audubon,* 101(4):44–53 (July–Aug. 1999).

France, Tom. "Bringing Grizzlies Back to the Bitterroots." *NWF EnviroAction,* 17(6):8–9 (June 1999).

A Future for the Grizzly: British Columbia Grizzly Bear Conservation Strategy. Victoria, BC: Ministry of Environment, Lands and Parks, June 1995. 16 pp.

Griffin, Donald R. *Animal Thinking.* Cambridge, MA: Harvard University Press, 1984.

Grinnell, George Bird. *The Cheyenne Indians: Their History and Ways of Life.* Lincoln, NE: University of Nebraska Press, 1972 (reprint).

Grizzly Bear Scientific Committee Reports 1995–1998. Victoria, BC: Ministry of Environment, Lands and Parks.

"Grizzlies in danger: Report." *National Post,* p. A4 (Feb. 26, 2000).

"Grizzlies studied in park." *Williams Lake Tribune,* p. A5 (Sept. 2, 1993).

Gunson, John and J. A. Nagy. 1990. *Management Plan for Grizzly Bears in Alberta.* Edmonton, AB: Department of Forestry, Lands and Wildlife, 1989. 164 pp.

Hamer, D. and S. Herrero. Grizzly bear food and habitat in the front ranges of Banff National Park, Alberta. *In International Conference on Bear Research and Management.* 7:199–213, 1987.

Haynes, B. D. and E. *The Grizzly Bear: Portraits from Life.* Norman, OK: University of Oklahoma Press, 1966.

Herrero, Stephen. *Bear Attacks: Their Causes and Avoidance.* New York: Nick Lyons Press, 1985.

———— and Andrew Higgins. "Human injuries inflicted by bears in British Columbia: 1960–1997." (*in press*)

Hittell, Theodore. *The Adventures of James Capen Adams, Mountaineer and Grizzly Bear Hunter of California.* North Stratford, NH: Ayer Company Publishers, 1972 (reprint).

Hornaday, William. *Our Vanishing Wildlife: Its Extermination and Preservation.* North Stratford, NH: Ayer Company Publishers, 1970 (reprint).

Hummel, Monte and Sherry Pettigrew. *Wild Hunters: Predators in Peril.* Toronto: Key Porter Books, 1991.

Hunting Regulations Summary 1999–2000. Whitehorse, YK: Ministry of Renewable Resources, 1999. 84 pp.

I'Anson, Bill. *Saving Berries for the Bears.* Victoria, BC: Ministry of Environment, Lands and Parks; 1995. 4 pp.

Interagency Grizzly Bear Committee. *Grizzly Bear Compendium.* Washington, DC: National Wildlife Federation, 1987. 540 pp.

Kasworm, W. F. *Cabinet Mountains grizzly bear study.* Annual Report April 1983–March 1984. Helena, MT: Montana Department of Fish, Wildlife and Parks. 50 pp.

Kelly, Cindy. "Bear Scare." *Explore,* June/July 1997. Issue 86, p. 18.

Khutzeymateen Study Report. Victoria, BC: Ministry of Environment, Lands and Parks, May 1992. 10 pp.

Knight, R. R. and L. L. Eberhardt. "Population dynamics of Yellowstone grizzly bears." *Ecology,* 66(2):323–324, 1984.

Kunelius, Rick. *Animals of the Rockies.* Canmore, AB: Altitude Publishing, 1983.

Leggett, Jeremy, ed. *Global Warming: The Greenpeace Report.* New York: Oxford University Press, 1990.

Leopold, Aldo. *A Sand County Almanac.* New York: Oxford University Press, 1949.

Lofroth, Eric. *Grizzly Bears in British Columbia.* Victoria, BC: Ministry of Environment, Lands and Parks. [nd.] 6 pp.

Legault, Steven. "Fall of the Grizzly." *Canadian Wildlife,* 2(4):12–19 (Sept.–Oct. 1996).

Lynch, Wayne. *Bears: Monarchs of the Northern Wilderness.* Vancouver, BC: Douglas & McIntyre, 1993.

MacArthur, Robert and Edward O. Wilson. *The Theory of Island Biogeography.* Princeton, NJ: Princeton University Press, 1967.

Macey, A. *Status Report on grizzly bear* Ursus arctos horribilis *in Canada.* Ottawa, ON: Committee on the Status of Endangered Wildlife in Canada, 1979.

MacHutchon, A. G., S. Himmer, and C. A. Bryden. *Khutzeymateen Valley Grizzly Bear Study: Final Report.* Wildlife Report No. R-25. Wildlife Habitat Research Report No. 31. Victoria, BC: Ministry of Forests, 1993. 105 pp.

Martinka, C. J. "Population characteristics of grizzly bears in Glacier National Park, Montana." *Journal of Mammalogy,* 55:21–29 (1974).

Marty, Sid. "Banff vs the Bears." *Canadian Geographic,* 117(1):28–39 (Jan./Feb. 1997).

McLellan, Bruce, Fred W. Hovey, Richard D. Mace, et al. "Rates and causes of grizzly bear mortality in the interior mountains of British Columbia, Alberta, Montana, Washington, and Idaho." *Journal of Wildlife Management,* 63(3):911–920 (1999).

McNamee, Thomas. *The Grizzly Bear.* New York: Alfred A. Knopf, 1984.

Miller, S. J., N. Barichello, and D. Tait. "The grizzly bears of the Mackenzie Mountains, Northwest Territories." Completion Report No. 3. Yellowknife, NWT: N.W.T. Wildlife Service, 1982.

Miller, S. D. and W. B. Ballard. "Homing of transplanted Alaskan brown bears." *Journal of Wildlife Management,* 46(4):869–876 (1982).

Mills, Enos. *The Grizzly, Our Greatest Wild Animal.* New York: Comstock Book Distributors, 1988 (reprint).

Mills, J. A. and Chris Servheen. *The Asian trade in bears and bear parts.* Washington, DC: World Wildlife Fund, 1991.

Mitchell, Alanna. "Building a home for the grizzlies to roam." *Globe and Mail,* p. A1 (Oct. 6, 1997).

Mortenson, Joseph. *Whale Songs and Wasp Maps: The Mystery of Animal Thinking.* New York: E. P. Dutton, 1987.

Mowat, Farley. *Sea of Slaughter.* Boston: Atlantic Monthly Press, 1984.

Murie, A. *The Grizzlies of Mount McKinley.* U.S. Department of the Interior, Scientific Monograph Series No. 14, 1981.

Murie, Olaus. *A Field Guide to Animal Tracks.* New York: Houghton Mifflin, 1982.

Murray, John A., ed. *The Great Bear; Contemporary Writings on the Grizzly.* Seattle: Alaska Northwest Books, 1992.

Nagorsen, David. *The Mammals of British Columbia: A Taxonomic Catalogue.* Victoria, BC: Royal British Columbia Museum Memoir No. 4, 1990.

Nagy, J. A., R. H. Russell, A. M. Pearson, S. Kingsley, and C. B. Larsen. *A study of grizzly bears on the barren grounds of Tuktoyaktuk Peninsula and Richards Island, Northwest Territories, 1974 to 1978.* Edmonton, AB: Canadian Wildlife Service, 1983. 136 pp.

Nagy, J. A. and A. G. MacHutchon. *Khutzeymateen Valley Grizzly Bear Study. Annual Progress Report—Year 1 (1989–1990) and Annual Working Plan—Year 2 (1990–1991).* Wildlife Working Report No. WR-48. Victoria, BC: B.C. Ministry of Environment, Lands and Parks, 1991.

Nagy, J. A., R. H. Russell, A. M. Pearson, et al. *Ecological studies of grizzly bears in the Arctic Mountains, Northern Yukon Territory, 1972 to 1975.* Edmonton, AB: Canadian Wildlife Service, 1983. 194 pp.

"1980–1995 Participation in Fishing, Hunting, and Wildlife Watching: National and Regional Demographic Trends." Report No. 96-5. Washington, DC: Division of Federal Aid, U.S. Fish & Wildlife Service, Sept. 1999. 84 pp.

1999 Alberta Guide to Hunting Regulations. Edmonton, AB: Department of Environmental Protection, 1999. 120 pp.

1999/2000 List of Canadian Wildlife at Risk. Ottawa, ON: Committee on the Status of Endangered Wildlife in Canada, 1999.

Nelson, Richard. *Make Prayers to the Raven: A Koyukon View of the Northern Forest.* Chicago, IL: University of Chicago Press, 1986.

Northwest Territories and Nunavut Summary of Hunting Regulations. Yellowknife, NWT: Department of Resources, Wildlife and Economic Development, 1999. 24 pp.

Obee, Bruce. *Grizzlies and Black Bears.* Vancouver, BC: Beautiful British Columbia Magazine Publications, 1996.

Patent, Dorothy Hinshaw. *The Way of the Grizzly.* New York: Clarion Books, 1987.

Peacock, Doug. *Grizzly Years.* New York: Henry Holt and Company, 1990.

Pearson, Arthur M. *The northern interior grizzly bear,* Ursus arctos. Ottawa, ON: Canadian Wildife Service Reprint Series No. 34, 1975. 86 pp.

Pynn, Larry. "Ban on sale of grizzly pelts urged." *Vancouver Sun,* p. A5 (July 11, 1995).

———. "The last journey home of Anderson the grizzly." *Vancouver Sun,* p. B6 (Nov. 9, 1999).

Quammen, David. "Island of the Grizzlies." *Audubon,* 97(2):82–91 (March–April 1995).

Read, Nicholas. "Bears' fierce image their biggest foe." *Vancouver Sun,* p. B2 (Nov. 4, 1995).

Regulations Synopsis 1999–2000: Hunting & Trapping. Victoria, BC: Ministry of Environment, Lands, and Parks, 1999. 96 pp.

Remington, Robert. "Killer highway creating animal ghetto in Banff." *National Post,* p. A1 (Feb. 9, 2000).

Renner, Ginger. *A Limitless Sky: The Work of Charles M. Russell.* Flagstaff, AZ: Northland Press, 1986.

Reynolds, H. V. and J. Hechtel. "Structure, status, reproductive biology, movement, distribution and habitat utilization of a grizzly bear population." *North Slope Grizzly Bear Studies,* Vol. 1 (July 1978–June 1979). Juneau, AK: Alaska Department of Fish and Game.

Russell, Andy. *Grizzly Country.* New York: Alfred A. Knopf, Inc., 1967.

Russel, R. H., J. W. Nolan, N. A. Woody, and G. Anderson. "A Study of the grizzly (*Ursus arctos*) in Jasper National Park, 1975–1979. Final Report. Ottawa, ON: Canadian Wildlife Service, 1979.

Safety Guide to Bears in the Wild. Victoria, BC: Ministry of Environment, Lands, and Parks, 1998. 4 pp.

Savage, Candace. *Grizzly Bears.* San Francisco: Sierra Club Books, 1990.

Schaffer, Mark L. Determining minimum viable population cases: A case study of the grizzly bear (*Ursus arctos*). PhD thesis, Duke University (Durham, NC), 1978.

Schoen, J. W. "Bear habitat management: A review and future perspective." *In International Conference on Bear Research and Management,* 8:143–154, 1990.

Servheen, Chris. "Grizzly bear food habits, movements, and habitat selection in the Mission Mountains, Montana." *Journal of Wildlife Management,* 47:1026–1035 (1983).

———. *Grizzly Bear Recovery Plan.* Second Review Draft. Washington, DC: U.S. Fish & Wildlife Service, 1992.

Seton, Ernest Thompson. *The Biography of a Grizzly.* New York: Century Publishing, 1900.

Sharpe, Sean. *Human-Bear Conflict in British Columbia: Draft Discussion Paper.* Victoria, BC: Ministry of Environment, Lands and Parks, 1996. 21 pp.

Sherwonit, Bill. "Bear Man of McNeil River." *National Wildlife,* 34(5):20–29 (Aug./Sept. 1996).

Storer, Tracy and Lloyd P. Tevis, Jr. *California Grizzly.* Lincoln, NB: University of Nebraska Press, 1955.

Struzik, Ed. "Scientists gain close view of grizzly bears." *Vancouver Sun,* pp. B1, B3 (Oct. 2, 1999).

"Suit contests grizzly hunt." *Calgary Herald,* p. B5 (Aug. 30, 1991).

Treadwell, Timothy and Jewel Palovak. *Among Grizzlies.* New York: Ballantine Books, 1997.

Troyer, W. A. "The brown bear of Kodiak Island." Kodiak, AK: U.S. Department of the Interior, Bureau of Sport Fisheries and Wildlife, Branch of Wildlife Refuges, Kodiak National Wildlife Refuge, 1969.

——— and R. J. Hensel. "Cannibalism in brown bear." *Animal Behaviour,* 10:231 (1962).

Turbak, Gary. "Lord of the Mountain." *Equinox,* Vol. III(6) No. 18:63–77 (Nov./Dec. 1984).

———. *Survivors in the Shadows.* Flagstaff, AZ: Northland Publishing, 1993.

———. "Getting Along with Griz." *Wildlife Conservation,* 96(6):44–53 (Nov.–Dec. 1993).

———. *Grizzly Bears.* Stillwater, MN: Voyageur Press, Inc., 1997.

———. "When Carnivores Clash." *National Wildlife,* 36(4):32–39 (June–July 1998).

Walker, Tom. *River of Bears.* Stillwater, MN: Voyageur Press, Inc., 1993.

Waller, John S. and Richard D. Mace. "Grizzly bear habitat selection in the Swan Mountains, Montana." *Journal of Wildlife Management,* 61(4): 1032–1038 (1997).

Ward, Paul and Suzanne Kynaston. *Wild Bears of the World.* London, England: Cassell plc., 1995.

Weber, Bob. "U.S. wants to import B.C. grizzly bears." *Vancouver Sun,* p. A23 (Aug. 18, 1997).

White, Don; Katherine C. Kendall, and Harold D. Pict. "Grizzly bear feeding activity at alpine army cutworm moth aggregation sites in northwest Montana." *Canadian Journal of Zoology,* 22(2):221–227 (Feb. 1998).

Wielgus, R. *Habitat ecology of the grizzly bear in the southern Rocky Mountains of Canada.* M.Sc. Thesis, University of Idaho (Moscow, ID), 1986.

Wilkinson, Todd. "Bear Necessities." *Audubon,* 101(4):54–61 (July–Aug. 1999).

Young, Donald D., Jr. and Thomas R. McCabe. "Grizzly bear predation rates on caribou calves in Northeastern Alaska." *Journal of Wildlife Management,* 61(4):1056–1066 (1997).

Index